Gracie's Girl

Also by Ellen Wittlinger:

Hard Love
What's in a Name
The Long Night of Leo and Bree
Razzle
Noticing Paradise
Lombardo's Law

Gracie's Girl

Ellen Wittlinger

Aladdin Paperbacks

New York London Toronto Sydney Singapore

First Aladdin Paperbacks edition April 2002

Text copyright © 2000 by Ellen Wittlinger

Aladdin Paperbacks
An imprint of Simon & Schuster
Children's Publishing Division
1230 Avenue of the Americas
New York, NY 10020

Also available in a Simon & Schuster Books for Young Readers
hardcover edition.

Designed by Steve Scott
The text of this book was set in Bembo
Manufactured in the United States of America
20 19 18 17 16 15 14 13 12 11
The Library of Congress has cataloged the hardcover edition as
follows:
Wittlinger, Ellen.
Gracie's girl / Ellen Wittlinger.
p. cm.
Summary: As she starts middle school, Bess volunteers to work on
the school musical in hopes of fitting in, but when she and a
friend get to know an elderly homeless woman, Bess changes her
mind about what is really important.
ISBN-13: 978-0-689-82249-0 (hc.)
ISBN-10: 0-689-82249-9 (hc.)
[1. Homeless persons—Fiction. 2. Shelters for homeless persons—
Fiction. 3. Schools—Fiction. 4. Family life—Fiction. 5. Identity—
Fiction.] I. Title.
PZ7.W78436Gr 2000   [Fic]—dc21   99-47318
ISBN-10: 0-689-84960-5 (Aladdin pbk.)
ISBN-13: 978-0-689-84960-2 (Aladdin pbk.)
0512 OFF

For my parents,
Doris and Karl Wittlinger

And for all the guests at
My Brother's Table,
Lynn, Massachusetts

With grateful thanks to my editor, David Gale,
his assistant, John Rudolph,
and my agent, Ginger Knowlton

Chapter One

It was the last week of the summer, and I felt like I should be getting *ready,* but there I was on Ethan's back porch again, playing Monopoly, just like most other days this summer. In fact, we were playing the same exact game we'd started in June. How many times the last three months had I landed in Jail and been glad to sit out a couple of my losing turns? Too many. Ethan was busy exchanging five-hundred-dollar bills for more hotels.

"Let's just say you win," I suggested. "In five days school starts. I want to do something *different.*"

Ethan stared at my treasonous face. "Bess! We said we'd play this game all summer!"

"We have. Almost."

"But you can't quit now. I've got hotels on Park Place and Boardwalk!"

"Yeah, and all the Railroads and all the greens and yellows and reds, too! I couldn't possibly win. I'm bankrupt!"

"Here, I'll lend you some more money," he said, giving me a fistful of hundred-dollar bills. That's what he always does. That's why we'll probably be playing this same game until we graduate from high school. Ethan doesn't really care about winning; he's just naturally good at games, and Monopoly is his favorite.

"Well, let's at least quit for today. We'll play some more tomorrow."

He wasn't happy, but I knew he'd give in. Ethan doesn't like to argue.

"Okay. But what else can we do? It's too hot to ride bikes."

"We could go to the pool," I said. Ethan never wants to go to the pool, but I thought maybe the heat would change his mind. He doesn't like wearing swimming trunks in public because he thinks he's fat.

"I told you, I don't want to go there again until I have my growth spurt." His mother told him he'd get thin again when he had his growth spurt, and he was waiting for it like an extra birthday. I hope he gets it before next summer so we can cool off once in a while.

"Is Janette home today? We could go over there."

"Are you kidding? It's Thursday afternoon, which is ballet *and* tennis."

Janette Silverman is my second best friend (after Ethan) and the shyest girl in our class. We might have all three been best friends except that Janette is too nervous to sit around playing games. And she never stays in one place very long. She's used to being busy; her mother has her booked up with lessons—ballet, singing, violin, tennis, swimming. And in the summer she has to take sailing

2

lessons every morning. I would die if I had to get up early even in the summer.

Sometimes Janette complains about having so much to do all the time. Once she told me, "My mother wants me to be a child prodigy. In anything—she doesn't care what. But I think I'm already too old." She chews her nails down to stumps.

Ethan was putting all his bills and property into perfect order so he'd be ready to monopolize me again tomorrow.

"What are you wearing to school next week?" I asked him.

He looked at me as if my body had been inhabited by aliens. "What do you mean? The same stuff I always wear."

"Ethan, we're starting middle school. You don't want to look like you're still going to Albertine Gustavson Elementary School, do you?"

He shrugged. "Sixth graders don't look that different from fifth graders."

"*Middle* school kids look different. You never notice anything."

"I do too. Besides, you don't look any different."

"Maybe not this minute, but I will. My mother bought me some new clothes. And I'm getting a haircut tomorrow afternoon and picking up my new glasses on Monday. They have thin silver frames and they're really cool." It was hard to believe I'd ever liked my old pink frames—they looked so childish now.

3

Ethan wasn't impressed. "Girls always do that stuff. Boys don't."

That made me mad. "Ethan Riley, I *never* did this before, and plenty of boys wear cool stuff to school. We've dressed like twin dorks for six years. It's time we started to look *interesting*."

"I am not a dork."

"You're the *biggest* dork!" I know that sounds mean, but Ethan and I always say that kind of stuff to each other. Besides, I could have told you what he'd say next.

"Who cares? Sweatpants are comfortable. Hey, your mom's home. Let's go to your house."

Ethan lives next door to me, so it's not exactly a hike to go back and forth. And he's crazy about my mother, probably because she thinks he's the neatest invention since toast.

I'd forgotten what our living room looked like until we walked in the front door.

"I think your closets exploded," Ethan said.

"It's rummage sale weekend at the church," I said.

"Oh, right, your mom was in charge of that last year, too."

"She's in charge of it *every* year. Like she doesn't have enough to do already between her job and helping out at the shelter. I've hardly seen her for weeks," I complained.

He was pulling old shoes out of a box and measuring them against his foot. "Couldn't somebody else do the rummage sale sometimes?"

I shook my head. "She *wants* to do it. So she can go through the stuff first and pick out things for the people at the shelter." Not that our house is ever what you'd call neat, but the weeks before the rummage sale things really get out of hand. The dining room fills up with garbage bags first, and by the last collection days the living room is starting to look like Goodwill, with old coffeemakers and ugly lamps, mismatched dishes, and busted-up game boxes stacked all over everything. And now the couch was piled high with clothes, too. Mom had obviously been rummaging herself.

"Hi, guys," Mom called from the kitchen. "Want some carrots?" Mothers never give up pushing vegetables.

"Could we make popcorn instead? Corn is a vegetable," I said. "How come you're home early?"

She came into the living room but had to finish chewing her carrot before she could speak. "I have to get the rest of these bags down to the church by five, but I want to check through them first for clothes for the shelter. How about you two giving me a hand, and then we'll make popcorn?"

"Sure!" Ethan volunteered. "I think it's so cool that you and Mr. Cunningham serve lunch at the shelter on Sundays. I wish my parents did something like that."

"Your parents are busy," Mom said, just to make Ethan feel better.

"Not as busy as *you*," I said, but they ignored me. Mom dumped a few garbage bags out on the floor and

5

explained to Ethan what she was looking for, mostly coats and warm sweaters. Some shoes, too.

"We don't go to the shelter every Sunday," Mom told Ethan. "More like every other week."

I felt like adding, *And then you go to meetings about it the rest of the time.* But I didn't. I know I shouldn't complain. I mean, she helps people who need her help. Maybe some Sunday I'll go stand in line at the soup kitchen and Mom will take a good look at me, too.

"You wouldn't think it was so great to have your parents out feeding other people if you had to stay home and make lunch for Willy," I told Ethan.

Mom threw a sweater onto the shelter pile and turned to stare at me. "What? Why are you making lunch for Willy? He's perfectly capable of taking care of himself."

"He always makes me some kind of bet or says I owe him for something."

"I'll speak to him," she said, but I knew she'd forget all about it. Mom is always talking about how you have to prioritize your responsibilities if you have a lot to do, and I learned a long time ago that Willy and I are not high on her priority list.

Willy's five years older than me, a junior in high school this year. It kills me when I hear girls say they wish they had an older brother. "Take mine," I tell them. "He's all yours." He was all right when we were younger, but as soon as he started high school he

6

stopped speaking. Now all he does is grunt and swear, unless he's talking to one of his friends on the telephone, of course. Then he's Mr. Hilarious.

"How come you never go?" Ethan asked me.

"Go where?" I wasn't paying attention.

"To the shelter with your parents."

"I don't like to," I said.

"How come?"

"I just don't, all right?" I poked through a big pile of junk and pulled out a worn blue cardigan with a hole in the elbow. "How about this? Is this good?"

"That looks fine, sweetie," Mom said, winking at me.

She knows it makes me uncomfortable to go to the Derby Street Shelter. It's in Atwood, but not near our house. It's in downtown Atwood, on the other side of the middle and high schools, in a kind of run-down area. Where our house is, it's pretty; all the houses have yards with trees and flowers and barbecue grills. But down there the buildings are close together, and some of the apartment windows are broken out. It makes me feel small to walk around there, like I don't belong.

When we were little, Willy and I used to go to the shelter with Mom and Dad because we were too young to stay home alone and it was hard to find a baby-sitter for Sunday afternoons. We'd sit back in the kitchen and eat soup and bread and salad. Dad would cook, which never seemed odd because he does most of the cooking at home, too. He loves cooking, which Mom says is one of his best qualities. Dad's a lawyer, but standing in the kitchen at the shelter, stirring a big kettle, he'd always say, "I should have been a chef."

After a while Willy and I decided we wanted to be out in front, where all the action seemed to be, at the serving line with Mom. Until we actually went out there.

It was kind of scary. I mean, a lot of the people looked okay, but some of them, when they got up close to you, smelled bad. I remember once there were two men in the back of the room having a loud argument about something, and some of the shelter people finally had to make them leave. One woman coughed all over her food, and her two little kids looked pretty snotty and sick, too. It was weird. I'd never been around people like that before. Some of them were downright crazy. You couldn't pretend they weren't. Even my parents couldn't.

Not that anybody ever hurt me or even touched me or anything. The last time we went, I guess I was about eight and Willy was thirteen. I was standing by the trash barrel, just daydreaming, and this old man looked me right in the eye and said, "Could you help me find my teeth? I dropped them in the barrel." Except without his teeth it sounded more like, "Would you hep me fine my teef? I dwopped dem in da barrow."

Now I realize I should have just told somebody about it; my mom or dad would've helped him look. But all I could think about was that big gummy mouth of his smiling at me, and me having to dig through the garbage to find his old yellow choppers.

So I started crying. I cried until Mom drove Willy and me home. And that was the last time we ever had to go to the shelter. Willy was thrilled to stay home and "baby-sit" for me, as long as I didn't bother him while he watched videos all afternoon.

I held up an enormous flowered skirt, about size 82. "Who buys this stuff, anyway?" I said. "I mean, I know poor people at the shelter need clothes, but why would anybody else want this junk?" I couldn't imagine wearing somebody's old, thrown-out clothes.

"Lots of people," Mom said. "You can start putting stuff back in the garbage bags now. I've got enough to take to Derby Street."

"But who?" I insisted.

"Well, there are people who just don't like to spend a lot of money on clothes. They think it's a shame to get rid of perfectly wearable clothes just because they aren't this year's styles. I feel that way."

"Yeah, but you wouldn't buy stuff at rummage sales."

"Of course I would! My favorite blouse is from last year's sale. I have a lot of clothes I've picked up at our sale."

I made a face. "Ethan, don't you tell a soul my mother wears used clothes." That's all I needed to ruin my new middle school image, the news that my mother wore somebody else's raggy, old outfits.

Ethan, of course, couldn't imagine why I objected to anything Alice Cunningham did. "What's the big deal? She looks fine." Saint Alice.

"Thank you, Ethan. Lots of people shop at rummage sales," Mom said. "Kids from the college come to pick up inexpensive, funky-looking outfits. People who like to stand out from the crowd, look a little different. And some people just can't afford to pay the prices they ask at the mall. They aren't homeless, but they don't want to waste their money on overpriced clothing."

As you can tell, my mother has a lot of opinions.

So do I. "Well, I don't get it. I mean, those clothes could be *dirty,* or something."

"That's why we own a washing machine," Mom said.

Ethan grinned. "I'm gonna go to the sale. It sounds like fun."

"Why?" I said. "All you ever wear is gray sweatpants and a navy blue sweatshirt."

He shrugged. "Maybe I'll change."

"Wait until Saturday," Mom suggested. "That's Bag Day. All you can stuff into a bag for one dollar. There's always lots left to choose from."

"Great," I said. "I'll come, too. I can help Ethan pick out a new housedress and a pair of fuzzy slippers." Ethan just laughed. I don't know why he doesn't have a million friends. He never gets mad at anybody, and he acts like everything you say is so darn funny.

Chapter Two

Bag Day. It sounded like a real waste of a Saturday to me. But Ethan couldn't wait to go, so I called Janette to see if she could come, too.

"I wish I could," she said. "My mother's picking me up after my voice lesson and we're going out for lunch and then to Springfield to a play."

"And you're sorry you can't go to Bag Day in the church basement instead? Maybe we should trade lives for a while."

She sighed. "I wish we could. I mean, I like my mom, but I wish she had more kids, or a job, or more friends or something, you know? I get tired of being her only child *and* her best friend."

I believed Janette that it was hard to have all that parental attention on you all the time—she could never get away with anything. Still, it must be kind of nice to have a mother who'd rather hang out with you than anybody else.

Ethan's mother doesn't have time for him, either. This is another thing we have in common—besides being dorks, I mean. His mother doesn't have a job, but she has about a million kids, all girls except for Ethan, some older and some younger, and all pains in the neck. She's always patting him on the head and saying stuff like, "Thank God for you, Ethan. You're the only one who doesn't give me gray hair."

So, of course, Ethan never does give her any trouble. Sometimes I think the two of us are really *lame*, being so good all the time.

"What are you looking for?" I asked Ethan. He was poking through piles of boys' clothing.

"I don't know. I thought maybe I could find some jeans or something."

"Jeans!" I was amazed. "You're not planning on becoming *cool*, are you?"

He blushed and looked around to see if anybody had heard me. "Come on, Bess. Almost everybody wears jeans now. Even you do."

"That's what I've been telling you! But don't get them here. Get new ones."

"I like the older ones. They're broken in already." He picked out a pair and started to try them on over his sweatpants. "Anyway, my mom has to buy so much stuff for my sisters. It costs too much to get new clothes for all of us."

He couldn't get the jeans pulled up over his other pants, of course. And he wouldn't look at me, either. I felt really stupid. When was I going to learn to think first, then talk? It hadn't occurred to me that Ethan's parents couldn't afford to buy him whatever clothes he wanted, the way mine could.

"There's a place to try things on," I told him. "The men's is over there. Maybe you should take a few pairs so you can figure out the right size."

"Okay." He smiled at me quickly and disappeared into the changing room.

While I was waiting for him to come out, I noticed these two girls, probably from the college, trying on all kinds of stuff. One had an old flowered dress pulled on over her leotard and tights. The top and bottom buttons she left undone. Then she layered some ancient beads around her neck and topped it off with a silly little hat with a veil.

"I love it!" the other girl screamed. "It's a riot! Help me find one."

They saw me watching them, and one of the girls threw a bright yellow scarf my way. "Here, put this in your hair—it's only good with really dark hair like yours!"

I picked it up carefully. It didn't look dirty or anything, but I didn't really want to tie a big yellow bow in my hair. I put it around my neck; it felt silky and soft.

The more I watched them, the more I liked the way they dressed up. It was just for fun. They weren't worrying about having the right logo or the same sweater that everybody else had this year. I remembered Mom saying kids who like to look different buy old clothes. *That* was what I could do. Instead of trying to look like the popular kids, which I never seemed to be able to do, anyway, I could look different *on purpose*. That would make kids notice me!

Ethan looked happy when he came out of the changing room. "I found two pairs that fit," he said.

"Great! Let's get a bag and fill it up. I want some stuff, too."

"You do?" He grinned. "Let's each get a bag, then. I want to get a lot."

So we each got bags and filled them to the top. Ethan got a few shirts and some sweaters, just regular-looking stuff, but they would definitely give him a new, nonfleece look. And once I got started, I went wild. I got two long skirts, one flowered and one patchwork, like a quilt. I bought some big tops and long sweaters that drooped down over my hands. I bought a pair of wide-legged pants that were orange plaid polyester. On the top of the bag were a bunch of scarves and a big black hat with a purple feather that swooped down low over the side.

"What are you going to do with all that stuff?" Ethan said. "Is it for Halloween or something?"

"I'm wearing it to school," I said.

Ethan's jaw dropped. "To school?"

"Any objection?"

"Gee, Bess. Just when I start to look normal, you'll look weird!"

"Well, if you're planning to be too *normal* to hang around with me now, you certainly don't *have* to."

"That's not what I mean. But nobody else dresses like that."

"That's the point! Don't you get it? Everybody will notice me. I'll be famous!"

Ethan shook his head. "I don't know why you'd want people to notice you. I hope *nobody* notices me."

"Well, I guess we're just different in that way," I said, fixing the hat on my head and throwing the feather around so it smacked him in the face.

"Cut it out. Listen, I have to get going. I promised my mom I'd watch the little girls this afternoon so she can clean out closets." Ethan, who never gave his mother a gray hair, paid his dollar and hurried out, hugging his precious bag to his chest.

I paid for my bag, too, then sat down to wait for Mom. Her shift was over at one o'clock. For a change we could have lunch together.

While I was sitting there waiting, I kept noticing this little old woman shuffling around, stuffing her bag so full, it was starting to rip down the side. She was bent over and had a big fluff of white hair all around her head. She had on an old pair of men's shoes, about three sizes too large for her. She caught me looking at her, and her eyes got real wide. She came over to me, holding up a huge dress. "Yessir, I used to wear a dress this big," she said to me. "I was a big girl, yessir, I was."

I gave her a weak smile, hoping she'd go away, but she didn't.

15

"How much do you think I weigh?" she asked, giving me a goofy grin.

I shrugged.

"Guess!" she demanded.

She wasn't much taller than I was, and she probably weighed less. Her arms were skinny sticks hanging out of an old gray coat. A coat, even though it was about 85 degrees outside.

"I don't know, maybe one hundred pounds," I said.

"Hah!" she laughed. "You lose! I weigh one hundred sixty pounds." She thought that was hysterical and finally walked off, laughing and dragging her busted bag.

When Mom came over, I pointed the woman out. "Look at that old lady. I think she's nuts. She's got about fifty things crammed in that bag. And she thinks she weighs one hundred sixty pounds."

"Oh, goodness. That's Gracie," Mom said. "She comes to the shelter for dinner on Sundays. I'll make sure nobody charges her for the clothes."

"It's only a dollar," I said.

"Bess, she doesn't have a dollar."

"How do you know?"

"She has no job, no family, no home. Where would she get money?"

I shrugged. "She must know somebody who gives her a little bit."

"I don't think so," Mom said.

"Is she crazy?"

16

"No, not really. She's a little odd, but living on the streets does that to you."

"I thought you said she lived at Derby Street?"

"No women live at Derby Street, Bess. There aren't any accommodations for them. They can eat at the soup kitchen, but not sleep there."

"Well, where does she sleep?"

Mom looked over at Gracie, who was still pushing clothing into her bag even though the side had split all the way down. "I don't know. She told me something once about a niece who wouldn't take her in, but I don't really know her story. It doesn't look like she has a home, does it?"

I was shocked. "But Mom, she's an old lady! She can't just sleep on the sidewalk somewhere!"

Mom put her arm around me. "Sweetie, some things aren't fair. No two ways about it. You never used to hear about homeless women, just men. But now there are all kinds of homeless people—men, women, and children."

"But can't you do something?" I asked. Surely my mother could help her; she helps everybody.

"I'm trying, Bess. That's why I've been going to so many evening meetings lately. A group of us from the shelter is trying to buy the old Emerson Hotel just around the corner from Derby Street. It wouldn't take much to turn it into a women's shelter. The hotel has been out of business for years, but the owner wants a lot of money for the building. We're working on it."

A little part of my brain was reminding me how much I hated for her to go to so many meetings at night. I tried to ignore it. "But that could take a long time," I said. "In another month it'll start to get cold outside."

"I know, sweetheart. I know." Mom sighed and looked at Gracie again. I looked, too. She'd pulled the enormous dress on over her coat and was tying a knitted muffler around her waist. She'd need all those layers before long. It made me feel kind of sick to think about her sleeping outside someplace, her big, old shoes poking into the sidewalk.

Chapter Three

The first day of school was a Tuesday. Every year they do that so you get tricked into thinking spending your whole week in school isn't so terrible—it's just four days, and there's not too much homework right away. But then along comes Week 2 and you remember: Oh, yeah, another year in prison.

I decided to start slowly with my new look. The haircut was shorter than I'd planned on, but my new glasses were great. I put on the patchwork skirt with a black T-shirt and tied the yellow scarf around my neck. I considered the hat, too, but chickened out when I imagined walking into a classroom full of strangers. For the first day the skirt and scarf would be enough to announce my new image.

Mom was pouring coffee down her throat when I came into the kitchen. She raised her eyebrows at the outfit but didn't say anything. Dad was getting ready to leave, but he stopped long enough to stare speechlessly, too.

Willy, who was drowning a huge bowl of Cheerios in milk, came up with a few words for me, though. "Holy crap! What are you wearing?"

"Willy!" Dad gave him his stern look.

"Now I'm *really* not giving you a ride," Willy said.

"I told you, I don't want to ride with you. I'd rather take the bus with Ethan and Janette." Willy'd had a driver's license and an old beat-up car for about two weeks, and all he could talk about was who could ride in it and who couldn't. Who cared?

"You know, Willy, if that's going to be your attitude, that car can sit on blocks in the garage until you're mature enough to drive," Mom said.

He dropped the spoon into the bowl and milk splashed everywhere. "I *paid* for the car. I bought it *myself!*"

"And we're paying your insurance. Unless you made enough money bagging fertilizer this summer to pay for *that* yourself?"

I could tell Willy wanted to keep up the argument, but Mom is known for making good on her threats, so he just picked up his bowl and stomped off into the living room.

"So, what do you guys think?" I threw one scarf tail over my shoulder.

"Pretty skirt," Dad said, shoving more papers into his briefcase. "Just don't trip over it."

"I won't. What do you think, Mom?"

"I think you'll get people's attention," she said. "Is that what you want to do?"

"Yeah, I guess so. I want to look different for a

change. Not like a grade school kid, but like . . . you know, a real person. Somebody who gets noticed. Besides, didn't you wear long skirts when you were a kid?"

"Not when I was eleven. And besides, that was the fashion then. Don't most girls just wear jeans to school now?"

"Yeah, but this way I'll stand out."

She smiled and ruffled my skirt. "Well, you look very nice, Bess, but don't be surprised if some kids are a little mean about your new look. Teenagers sometimes feel threatened by people who choose to be different from the norm."

Mom knows these things because she's a counselor at the high school, and she deals with teenagers' problems all the time. Which is sort of annoying. I mean, she's always giving me all this advice, which is probably pretty good advice, because it's her job and everything, but sometimes it just doesn't seem right for me. I feel like saying, *Maybe that advice helped some other kid, but we're not all the same. And, anyway, I don't want to know what some book says counselors should tell students. I want you, my mother, to listen to me, Bess, and help me figure out what I should do.*

"Do you want me to give you a ride this morning?" she asked. "You can't ride your bike in a skirt." Mom doesn't have to be at work until nine o'clock, and she likes to spend the hour after the rest of us leave reading

21

the newspaper, drinking coffee, and putting too much butter on her toast while there's nobody around to see her do it. She always says it's her one hour a day of indulgence.

"I'm fine. I'm taking the bus." I gave her a hug, and she winked. The minute I was outside I felt funny, though, like *everything* was different instead of just my clothes. For a minute I wondered if I ought to go back and change into jeans.

But I didn't. I could see Ethan and Janette were already at the bus stop, so I wouldn't have time, anyway. Janette lives about three blocks away and can get on before us, but she hates getting on alone, so unless it's really cold out, or Ethan and I want to ride our bikes, she walks the three blocks and faces the bus bozos among friends. I don't blame her, especially this year.

This was an earlier bus than the one we used to take to Albertine Gustavson Elementary. Even high school kids ride this bus, which goes all the way downtown and stops at both the middle and high schools. Which meant it would be full of kids we didn't even know.

Ethan, of course, took my new look in stride. "Don't trip on your skirt," was all he said. How come everybody thought I hadn't learned to walk yet?

But Janette was a little upset. "Bess, it's a pretty skirt, but everybody will stare at you, won't they? And the yellow scarf is kind of . . . *yellow*."

"Let them stare. I want them to." I wished I felt as

confident as I sounded. "I'll meet lots of people if they notice me."

"Why do you want to meet more people?" Janette asked. "You know us."

"We'll *all* meet new people. We'll be popular. It'll be fun!" Janette looked worried. "Do you like my new glasses?" I asked her.

"Oh, I do like them. They're very cool."

That was good. My idea was that since the glasses were cool, they would help me get away with the rest of it.

Janette knows what's cool and what isn't. She'd dressed the right way for years, although it didn't really matter, because the way she acted nobody noticed her, anyway. She was always dashing into the bathroom, or staring into her locker, or sitting in the back of the class, hiding behind somebody tall. And you couldn't talk to her about it, either. She'd get embarrassed and run away. It was like having a squirrel for a friend; you always had to be careful not to scare her off.

It was probably harder for Janette to get on that bus behind me than for me to get on in the first place. Of course, I *did* trip on the skirt, climbing up the bus stairs. Ethan didn't say anything, but a bunch of seventh-grade girls in the front knocked themselves out laughing.

"What's *she* supposed to be? A fortune-teller? Is this Halloween?"

There was no place to sit, so we had to stand in the aisle about halfway back. Those same stupid girls kept turning around to make comments about my clothes. I didn't even know them. Ethan and I pretended we couldn't hear them; he told me some story about his little sisters throwing their breakfasts at each other, but it was hard to pay attention. What if this went on all day? What if the kids I knew laughed at me? What if Janette passed out on the floor of the bus to escape?

By the time we got to the middle school I felt like I had a rock in my stomach. The three of us walked into the building huddled together like one nervous lump. There were teachers in the hallway telling everybody where to go, and, fortunately, it was too hectic and jammed for anybody to notice anybody else very much. All the older kids were talking loudly, and banging their lockers, and basically just acting like they were all comfortable being in this big, overcrowded place. Meanwhile the sixth graders stood around looking worried and dopey until the vice principal came down and herded us into the auditorium so he could drill a bunch of new rules into us. Then we got our schedules and had to figure out where all the different rooms were. It's so embarrassing not to know anything. But at least everybody was too busy being lost to laugh at my clothes.

Atwood Middle School is a big building with three floors, nothing at all like Albertine Gustavson, which is all on one level. A lot of the kids at Gustavson were related to each other, or at least lived in the same neighborhoods, so by the time you were in the third grade, you felt like you knew everybody. Everything was familiar. At the middle school even the kids I already knew seemed like strangers.

At least I had lunch the same time as Ethan and Janette. By then Janette was practically hysterical, although you could only tell by her eyes, big and round and searching for an exit. "There's not one person I know in my first three classes," she said.

"I thought Sam Milner and Paul Sokolov were in that math class," Ethan said.

Janette shivered. "They're boys!"

"So is Ethan," I pointed out. "You talk to him."

"Ethan's different," she said, blushing. Ethan grinned, like that was a compliment, but I had my doubts.

I compared our schedules. "At least we're all in English together after lunch."

Ethan was wolfing down two ham sandwiches. "You'll be happy to know Kimberly Pringle says she's in our English class, too. I saw her this morning."

"Oh, great." Kimberly was my least favorite person from Albertine Gustavson. She could never shut up, and all she wanted to talk about was herself. She always knew exactly what to wear, too. If anybody noticed my new look, Kimberly would.

The lunch bell rang in about twenty minutes, before we could even finish our gloppy puddings. And there was no recess here, either. I was beginning to think there was just too much *school* at the middle school.

We had a disagreement over where the English class-room was (I was so sure we turned *right* at the principal's office), and the room was already pretty full when we got there.

"Hi, Bess!" somebody yelled across the classroom. "What are you supposed to be? A hippie?" I knew it was Kimberly Pringle before I even turned around. She laughed, and a group of kids I didn't know laughed with her. It figured.

"What's she supposed to be?" Ethan said to me. "An idiot?"

Meanwhile, I hardly recognized *her*.

"Ethan, why didn't you tell us she looked like that?" I whispered.

"Like what?" He really didn't know. Janette rolled her eyes.

Over the summer Kimberly had grown about a foot taller, her hair had grown about two feet, and her chest was keeping up with her other body parts. Plus, she was wearing a shirt that kept falling down over her shoulders so that her bra straps showed!

"You didn't notice?" I asked Ethan. "She's got, you know ... boobs!"

Ethan turned purple. He's not too crazy about this kind of conversation. "Bess!"

"She has a boyfriend, too," Janette said. "I heard Kate Patrick say Kimberly was going with Russell Turner all summer."

"Russell Turner! He's a seventh grader!" I said, perhaps a bit too loudly.

"Quiet!" yelled a voice from the front of the room. Mrs. Moss had her eyes on the three of us. "I can tell who the troublemakers are going to be by the end of the first day, so keep your eyes up here and your mouths closed!"

I thought Janette would faint dead away before Mrs. Moss turned her glare onto somebody else. And wouldn't you know Mrs. Moss was one of those imaginative teachers who seat classes alphabetically, which meant that Ethan and Janette, as usual, ended up in the last row over by the windows, which happens to be my favorite place to sit, so I can at least glimpse the outside world once in a while, and I ended up at the back of the first row, in a dark corner, Cunningham behind five or six As and Bs.

When class was over, the girl in front of me stood up and smiled. "Where'd you get your skirt? It's really pretty."

"The rummage sale at my church," I said. She looked a little shocked, so I explained. "A lot of college kids buy their clothes there so they can look different from everybody else."

"Oh, that's kind of neat. My name's Suzanne, by the way."

"I'm Bess."

"Well, let me know if you go to any more rummage sales. Maybe I'll go along."

"Okay, I will."

I knew it! It was going to work! People *see* you when you stand out from the crowd. They want to get to know you.

Well, some of them do. Just then some lummoxy kid bumped into me on purpose, and I dropped my books. "Hey, look, it's Annie Oakley! Where's your horse, Annie? Where's your gun?"

His shaved-headed buddy laughed and started to walk bowlegged, like he'd just gotten off a horse. They were making such a racket, whinying and shooting pretend rifles, that other kids looked over at me, and some of them laughed, too. Not loud or anything, but I could feel my face getting hot and red. Who'd want to be friends with jerks like that, anyway? Still, just knowing kids were laughing at me again made me feel dizzy.

In a minute Ethan and Janette were standing next to me, and I started to feel better. Probably people were laughing at those dumb boys, not *me*.

Janette sneezed about four times in a row. "My mother says this is my fall allergies, but I think I'm just allergic to school."

"Well, at least it's over for today," Ethan said. "Anybody remember where the sixth-grade lockers are?"

"Down that hall," I guessed.

"No, we're on the third floor," Janette said. "We have to go down to the second." I figured she was probably right. Janette pays attention to things like that.

So we trudged down the stairs and headed toward the green lockers that identified us as the babies of the school. But before we got to the lockers, we passed a hand-lettered sign that I realized right away would be the key to changing our dull lives at Atwood Middle School. Here was something that would transform us into active, interesting, fun people. People everybody would want to know.

MIDDLE SCHOOL MUSICAL
AUDITIONS FRIDAY.
EVERYONE WELCOME!

I stopped our mopey group in front of the announcement. "This is it! This is what we'll do!" I said, turning to my friends, full of enthusiasm.

Ethan closed his eyes and groaned. Janette took one look at the sign and ran into the nearest girls' bathroom.

Chapter Four

I held on to Janette's wrist while the three of us stood outside the auditorium doors Friday afternoon. I knew if I let her go, she'd disappear faster than a doughnut in front of Homer Simpson.

"My mother will kill me if I miss my jazz dance lessons!" Janette insisted.

"You hate jazz dance," I pointed out.

"Yes, I do. Because you have to stand up in front of people and dance. What do you think I'd have to do in a musical?"

"But this would be different. You'd be onstage with forty or fifty other people and you'd be singing, too." A look of horror illuminated her face, and I knew I hadn't chosen a convincing argument.

"Okay. Go to your lesson. But don't blame me when Ethan and I are popular and you still don't know anybody."

"I'll still know *you*, won't I?" she said.

"Sure," Ethan said. "And we'll introduce you to all these real popular kids we're going to be hanging out with now. Probably by tomorrow, if they're lucky." Ethan didn't have 100 percent confidence in my plan, either.

Janette took off, and I started to open the door, but Ethan pushed it shut again. "Wait a minute, Bess. I know you really want to do this, but I can't sing *or* dance. How can I be in a musical?"

I had to admit that was true. Ethan's voice sounds kind of like bad brakes just before a car wreck. I read the sign on the door again.

"Look. You don't have to be *in* the musical. You can sign up to work on the crew, to help build the sets and paint things. You could do that, couldn't you?"

Ethan thought about it a minute. "I guess I could," he said. "But is working on the crew cool enough? I mean, will I be able to meet the really *popular* kids, do you think?"

I punched him in the arm. "You know what I mean. They don't have to be really popular, just more popular than us. Come on, Ethan, don't you think we ought to meet some other kids?"

"Expand our horizons, you mean?"

I had to laugh. That's what Janette's mother is always telling her to do. Expand her horizons. I wondered if she knew that Janette had a hard time even making eye contact with her two best friends. Forget the horizons.

"Yes, that's exactly what I mean," I said.

As we walked into the auditorium, Ms. Plumbly, the dramatic arts teacher, was hollering. "If you're signing up for crew, the sheet is on the back table. If you're audition-ing for a part, boys go backstage with Mr. Henry to learn the song. Girls stay in here with me and we'll learn a dance. Then you'll switch places."

Kids were milling around all over the theater. Ms. Plumbly has a reputation for putting on terrific plays, and I'd heard kids talking about wanting to be in the musical all week.

"If you don't get a part, please don't be upset," Ms. Plumbly begged, but you could tell she knew we would be, anyway. "I need lots of backstage help, and you'll learn a great deal about the theater doing that, too. Okay. Girls up onstage."

Ethan signed up for the crew and then took a seat in the back of the auditorium. "Go on," he said. "I'll wait for you."

All of a sudden my legs felt weak, like I could hardly walk up the steps to the stage. My hands got sweaty, and when I looked at all the other potential musical stars around me, my stomach flip-flopped, too. There were about fifty other girls crowded onto the stage, some of them wearing short shorts and black eye makeup, or little halter tops and ballet shoes. They looked about twenty-three years old. I wore jeans and sneakers instead of a long skirt because I thought that would be better for the audition. Even when I think I'll look like everybody else, I'm wrong. Which is why I shouldn't even try.

When I looked out at Ethan, he waved. I wished he weren't out there watching me.

I went to the back of the pack. I was never much of a

dancer. Mom took me to tap lessons for about two months, but I kept humming the wrong music and getting everybody mixed up, including myself. I'm much better at singing, but I had to get through the dance audition before I could prove that.

"Bess!" An all-too-familiar voice called out. There was Kimberly Pringle, in a cute little outfit that looked more like a swimming suit than anything else, her long blond hair pulled up into a ponytail waterfall. "I never thought *you*'d try out for the musical!" she yelled. Twenty girls turned around to stare at me.

"Surprise!" I said, forcing myself to grin.

"Pay attention, girls!" Ms. Plumbly said. The pianist started to play a song I recognized, "Put on a Happy Face."

"Are we doing *Bye Bye Birdie*?" I asked the girl next to me, who apparently thought circling her eyes with black chalk was a surefire way to get a part.

She looked me over. "Those of us who get in are," she said.

Thanks. Could she tell I was clumsy just by looking at me? I bent down and pretended to tie my shoe, then slipped over to the other side of the group. At least I didn't have to stand next to her.

The dance Ms. Plumbly taught us seemed way too long and difficult to me, but I could tell some of the girls already knew how to do the steps. The dancers. The ones who had the same hip joints as Barbie. The ones who could hold their legs straight up over their heads so their knees were practically stuck in their ears. I danced more like a Cabbage Patch doll. How was I going to stand up here by myself with everybody watching me and plod through this dance? The thought of it made my scalp itch.

Step, step, step, kick! Turn. Right hand up, out, turn … Step, kick, step, turn, no, wait, that's not it. Boom. I bumped smack into another girl. She apologized, so at least I knew I wasn't the only one who was confused.

By the time Ms. Plumbly told us to go sit down, I was panting. And I still didn't know which way to turn when. If Ethan hadn't been sitting there watching, I would have sneaked out that minute, but I didn't want him to think I was a quitter.

Ethan has this idea that I'm sort of fearless, which probably comes from that time in second grade when I fell off the jungle gym and knocked two teeth out. He was very impressed that I didn't cry about it, and that I climbed back up to the top the very next day. They were baby teeth; it wasn't that big a deal. Still, I kind of like it when he tells people, "Bess will do *anything*."

"Get a drink if you need one, then we'll start getting you up onstage in groups of five," Ms. Plumbly said. "By the way, if there's anyone here who'd be interested in taking on the job of stage manager, please let me know. I need someone who's a quick learner and very organized. It's a big job with a lot of responsibility."

I raised my hand before I'd really thought it through. A big job meant everybody would know who I was. I like organizing my books and my CD collection, so I'd probably be good at this, too. And, of course, the number one reason to be the stage manager: I wouldn't have to get up on that stage and dance.

"Are you interested?" Ms. Plumbly asked, seeing my hand.

"I think so. I'm a pretty quick learner."

"Oh, she'd be good at *that*," said Kimberly, speaking right up from the front row, just where I would have guessed she'd plunk herself down. "I've known Bess for years. She's good at behind-the-scenes kinds of things." Kimberly smiled in my direction, as though she knew she was doing me a big favor, but I didn't really need to thank her.

I couldn't believe it! She'd made me sound like a doofus—like the only things I'd be capable of doing were shoving furniture around and hiding behind the curtain. She didn't know anything about me! It was almost enough to make me change my mind and do the dance audition, anyway. Almost, but not quite.

"Good," Ms. Plumbly said. "I'm glad to find someone I can count on. You won't need to stay today, then. Come to my office Monday after school and we'll discuss your responsibilities, all right? By the way, what's your name?"

"Bess," I said, stumbling out of my row, over everybody's feet. I couldn't wait to get out of there.

"Bess Cunningham," Kimberly shouted out, helpful as always. If only I could find the time to pull out every glowing strand of her hair by the roots.

Ethan was waiting for me at the back door. "What made you decide to be the stage manager? I didn't know you were interested in that."

"I didn't, either," I said.

"So," he said, "I guess you can't dance."

"At least I can sing," I grumbled, giving him a dirty look.

He laughed. "Let's go to my house and play Monopoly."

"Why not?" Boring. My life was hopelessly boring.

Chapter Five

By Monday I still hadn't gotten up the nerve to wear my hat with the purple feather. But I had come across some old Valentine decorations in the bottom of my Dollar Bag—a thin red wire with little hearts dangling from it—that looked great tied around my forehead like a sweatband. My hair fluffed out in a pretty way, which made me wish I hadn't cut it. I wore my flowered skirt and a red top that was longer in the back than the front. Maybe I didn't look like those college girls, but I certainly would stand out from all the girls in their jeans-and-T-shirt uniforms.

I noticed a few kids rolling their eyes when they walked toward me in the hallway, but they were eighth graders, so who cared? Nobody I knew said anything until English class. Then Suzanne turned around and said, "Where do you come up with these outfits? I wouldn't have the guts to wear stuff like that, but it looks really cool on you."

Finally, someone who appreciated me. I shrugged. "It's just stuff I find around. I like looking unusual."

"You should meet my friend Anna. She likes to dress

up in crazy stuff, too, only she mostly does it at home. She's not as brave as you are."

As I walked out the door of the classroom, I adjusted my headband and smoothed my skirt, glad not to be a coward like Anna. Kimberly Pringle followed me, but she was not quite as complimentary about my new look as Suzanne. "For goodness' sake, Bess, aren't you overdoing it a little? You look like you're on your way to Woodstock."

I tried to ignore her, but for some reason standing next to Kimberly with her ton of swirly hair that hung down below her teeny, little skirt made me feel as dorky as I had last year.

"Your haircut's not bad, though. I could show you how to fix it, if you want," she said, flashing me her big, gooey smile.

There was something very suspicious about Kimberly Pringle paying so much attention to me. "I can't talk now," I told her. "I have to go see Ms. Plumbly about being stage manager for *Bye Bye Birdie*."

Kimberly kept following me. "Oh, I know. That's such a responsible job! You'll practically be the boss of the whole thing, after Ms. Plumbly, of course. I'm glad I talked you into it, aren't you?"

What? "I volunteered for it," I reminded her.

"Well, sure, but I mean, I vouched for you and every-thing."

I'm sure that made all the difference, since Ms.

Plumbly didn't know either one of us. This must be why Kimberly suddenly wanted to be my hairdresser; she thought that in my powerful position as stage manager I might be able to do something for her. I'd be lucky to figure out the basics of the job, let alone help out Princess Pringle.

"Did you get a good part?" I asked her.

"Didn't you see the cast list? I'm Ursula—that's the third-best girl's part. They gave the two female leads to eighth graders, which I guess is fair, although I would have been great as Kim, which is the best part, and, of course, it's even my name, so . . ."

She couldn't stop flapping her jaws. What a joy to think I'd be spending the next nine weeks working with Beauty and the Blabber.

"See you," I said, escaping into Ms. Plumbly's office.

At first I didn't even notice Ms. Plumbly sitting at her desk; she's not very tall, and the desk was piled high with papers and folders and books that looked like they were ready to slide onto the floor any minute. She peeped up from behind the stacks. "Oh, hello . . . Bess, isn't it? I hope you're here because you still want to be my stage manager."

I nodded. "I do."

Ms. Plumbly didn't look twice at my outfit. "Good. There's lots to be done." She started digging through one of the shorter piles on the desk, picked out a heavy folder, and handed it up to me. "Here's the script. You'll need to know it backwards and forwards. Not just one part, like each of the actors, but the whole thing. Do you have a good memory?"

I nodded. "For everything but dates. I can never remember if something happened in 1746 or 1647."

Ms. Plumbly smiled. "Well, there aren't any dates in *Bye Bye Birdie*. You'll come to all the rehearsals and listen to what I tell everybody to do, where to stand, how to stand, when and where to sit, when the songs begin, and on which side of the stage every character enters and exits. Everything. Your job is to take notes and forget nothing. You are my eyes and ears backstage. You need to know how to raise and lower the curtains, which backdrops to pull down when, where all the scenery goes, and what props are needed in each act. You'll have help doing it, of course, but *you* need to *know* it. Any questions?"

It sounded like way too much for one mere sixth grader to remember. "Not yet," I said hesitantly.

She laughed and twirled a little in her chair. "I'm sure you'll have plenty once we get started. I'm glad to get another sixth grader to train—then you'll be with me for three years, just like your predecessor, Liz Peterson, who graduated last spring. I promise you, this will be the most fun you've ever had working like the devil. Okay?"

"Okay." Now I have to do this for three years?

"By the way, I like your crown of hearts."

That was cool! "Thanks."

40

"So, I'll see you Wednesday afternoon in the Little Theater, and every Monday, Wednesday, and Friday after that." She stood up and gave me a little salute; I was dismissed. This could definitely be fun.

Kimberly was still standing outside Ms. Plumbly's office when I came out, as if she'd been waiting for me. "The guy who got the part of Birdie is *so* cute. He's an eighth grader and he's even better-looking than Russell Turner! Isn't this *so* exciting?" She grabbed my arm and twisted it like a washcloth.

I know, I wanted people to notice me, but Kimberly Pringle? I'd had all I could take of her for one day. "I have to meet Ethan down by the freshmen lockers," I said. I was pretty sure that would get rid of her: Even though Ethan had traded his sweatpants for jeans, he was no Russell Turner. It worked.

"I don't know what you see in Ethan, Bess. If you're going to be *somebody* in this school, you need to choose your friends more carefully."

I feel bad that I didn't say something mean back to her, like, *I do choose carefully—that's why I don't hang around with you,* or something like that. The thing is, it surprised me when she said that about my being *somebody*, and I hate to admit it, but it made me feel kind of proud. Besides, as annoying as Kimberly is, I knew that kids who walked by and saw me talking to her in the hallway were probably noticing me for the first time. That's just how things are in middle school. And I was determined that

41

this year people were going to notice me. If it took talking to Kimberly once in a while to help me toward my
goal, I'd just have to do it.

I did feel a little disloyal to Ethan, though, even if
he'd never know.

By Wednesday I'd gotten up the nerve to wear the
black hat with the purple feather. I wore the orange
polyester pants, too, with a big black top to sort of pull
the whole thing together. Today was the first rehearsal
for *Bye Bye Birdie*, and I wanted to make an impression
on the cast and crew members so they wouldn't forget
who I was.

I waved good-bye to Dad as he was going out the
door, and he started to wave back but then stopped and
stared, silently. Mom didn't say a word, either—I had a
feeling they'd made a pact. Fortunately Willy had left
early, so I didn't have to hear his stupid comments.

At the bus stop Ethan just rolled his eyes and said,
"What next?"

But Janette was upset. "Just promise me you'll never
come to my house looking like that," she said. "I mean it.
If my mother ever saw you wearing that, she'd never let
me hang around with you again."

"Why? You're not wearing it. I am."

"She thinks if you don't shop at Ann Taylor and J.
Crew you shouldn't be allowed to tread the earth. She
thinks girls who wear black are stoners, and people who

wear headbands are dropouts. And she thinks all those things are contagious. So promise me."

I promised never to disturb Janette's mother's warped view of reality, then climbed onto the bus to receive the insults of my peers. People certainly recognized me now.

What I learned from that day was that you can go too far with a good idea. And if you do, the only person who won't desert you is Ethan. The minute we took a seat on the bus, the jerk in back of us grabbed my hat and threw it to another jerk, and when I stood up to get it back, the bus driver yelled at me to sit down. By the time I got it back—the bus driver wouldn't let anybody off until I had it in my hands—it was all dusty, and the feather was cockeyed. Darn it, why did so many kids think it was their business what I wore to school?

Janette fled the minute the driver opened the door, but Ethan helped me clean up my hat. "I think you might be asking for trouble with this thing," he warned me.

"But I *like* it," I whined. I knew Ethan was probably right, but I couldn't give up that easily, could I? Just because there are a bunch of morons on the bus?

Down at the lockers Suzanne came up with her friend Anna. "I told her you'd have something weird on today," Suzanne boasted.

Anna just looked embarrassed.

"The hat got a little wrecked on the bus," I said.

"That hat won't make it through the day, Bess," Ethan predicted before going off to his first class.

"Oh, well, at least it got people's attention, huh?" Suzanne said. "Anna, you should wear your stuff like this to school."

"My dad would kill me," she said, but she smiled a little.

"What do your parents say about it?" Suzanne asked me.

"Not much. They're pretty busy. Clothes aren't a big deal with them." And neither is anything else I do.

"Lucky," Anna said.

"Yeah, I guess," I said, though I wasn't so sure.

In first period Mr. Milton warned me I couldn't wear my hat during class—he said it was a distraction to the other students—so I put it on the floor. I decided I'd just wear it between classes in the hall. But of course people kept grabbing it off my head and I'd have to chase them, and once I accidentally knocked down a really small sixth-grade boy. Finally Mrs. Falucci, the principal, confiscated it until school was out for the day. I didn't even care. I was tired of it by then, anyway.

Some of the kids throwing the hat around were really mean about it and said things like, "It belongs to that clown who thinks every day is Halloween." Even though the girls who said it are not people I'd ever want to be friends with, it hurt that they said it loud enough for me to hear them. I mean, is it a law that seventh graders have to hurt sixth graders' feelings?

I got the hat back before going over to play rehearsal

44

with Ethan and Janette—that was what I really wanted it for, anyway. I'd talked Janette into coming with us on Wednesdays, her only unscheduled afternoon, to work on scenery with Ethan. She'd brought a big old shirt of her father's to wear over her clothes so she wouldn't get paint or dirt on anything, an idea that had her mother's stamp all over it.

When we walked into the auditorium, Ms. Plumbly had her arms in the air, pointing people this way and that way, trying to get things under control. Everybody was too excited to listen to her, though.

Finally she got tough. "HEY! I want all the scenery people, props people, and stagehands out of here!" She pulled on the arm of a slump-shouldered boy with spiky hair who was wearing a blue deliveryman's shirt, the kind that has a name tag sewn onto the front. "This is Jake—don't be fooled by the 'Bruce' badge. Backstage people follow Jake. He's the set director. He'll show you The Zone, the cellar underneath the gym, where the flats are painted and the props are stored."

People began milling around, following Jake. I wasn't sure where I was supposed to be.

"Ms. Plumbly?" I called.

"Oh, Bess, good. You need to learn the ropes. Tell you what . . . Jake, wait a minute."

Jake stopped at the door and waited, like he was a robot under Ms. Plumbly's control. For some reason I just liked him right away, even though, standing there with his hands in the back pockets of his low-slung pants, he looked kind of like a sourpuss. A cute sourpuss.

Ms. Plumbly dragged me over to where he was standing. "Jake, this is Bess, the new stage manager. I want her to hang out with you and Amy this afternoon. Show her how everything works."

Jake nodded without smiling, and Ms. Plumbly turned to me. "Amy is props manager—she's already down in The Zone. Once I get the actors up on their feet, you'll be in here with me, but for now I think you'll learn more tagging along after Jake." Seemed like a good plan to me. I put my hat back on, just to make sure Jake knew that I, too, was a maverick, an individualist, a thespian.

Jake was tall and thin and took giant steps; the rest of us had to run to keep up with him. He crossed the lawn to the back of the gymnasium and went down a stairwell I'd never even noticed before. Then he opened a steel door to reveal a secret paradise hidden beneath Atwood Middle School. The Zone.

Never would I have imagined such a place was right here under my nose, or rather, under my feet. The space was huge, although there was so much stuff down there, you could only walk through on small pathways. The cement walls had been painted over and over again, with cartoons and names and graffiti. There were scenery flats piled along the back walls, and old furniture of all colors and sorts lined up on the floor. There were tools and paint cans and jars full of brushes. There were lamps and dishes and old television sets. A forest of cardboard trees marched down one aisle, and several pairs of wings flew from an overhead pipe. A papier-mâché dog guarded the entrance. It was wonderfully bizarre.

"Okay. We're painting over those *Peter Pan* flats back there," Jake called. "Let's move them outside, where we got room." Ethan and some of the other kids grabbed hold of the flats and started lugging them outside. Janette stood behind me and tried to disappear.

"When the weather's good, we paint outside," Jake explained. "Otherwise, we use The Zone Annex, that old shed across the parking lot. It's for overflow flats, but there's room to work in there, too. We don't put any heavy furniture back there because it's so far from the auditorium."

I figured Jake must be an eighth grader, but he seemed even older than that because he knew so much about everything. "Amy!" he yelled.

A girl with straggly brown hair pulled back in a clip stuck her head out of a door in the back of the room. "Yeah?"

"Plumbly wants you to show this kid around."

"Me?"

"That's what she said."

I was disappointed, but I didn't want to argue and make him like me even less.

"Is she costumes?" Amy asked.

47

"No, she's stage manager."

Even dressed in orange pants and a goofy hat, I felt completely invisible. The odd thing was, Jake *did* notice Janette, even though by this time she was hiding behind an eight-foot palm tree. "Come outside with me," he told her. "You can paint the park backdrop." He said it like it was an honor or something.

"Come on back here," Amy ordered as I watched Janette mutely follow Jake out the door.

The little back room where Amy was working was hung floor to ceiling with costumes, hundreds of them, everything from Shakespearean gowns to gorilla suits. "Wow," I said, fingering a nun's habit. "Look at all this stuff."

"Yeah, it's a mess. What's your name?"

"Bess."

"Sixth grader?"

I nodded.

"Don't take your hat off down here. It'll get claimed for a costume." At first I thought she was laughing at me, but she wasn't. Amy didn't really laugh much. "I'm waiting for a costume manager to show up, preferably somebody who's been in this room before. I know we moved a box of telephones in here last year, but now I can't find them."

"Why do you need telephones?"

"We need twenty-five phones for one of the songs. I'll make you a copy of the props list. Since you don't have to be onstage for a week or so, you can help me locate stuff. Some of it will be down here, and some we'll have to come up with ourselves. For instance, I need a guitar. An old one, in case it gets wrecked. Acoustic, not electric. Know where we can get one?"

"My dad used to think he was Bob Dylan. Maybe we could use his old guitar."

She actually smiled. "Great. And you know what else you could do for me? This weekend, go to Donut Heaven and ask them if they'll donate a couple boxes of doughnuts the weekend of the play. We need them for the breakfast scene. And maybe some juice packs, too. While you're at it, see if they'll donate some stuff for the cast party, too."

"Do they usually do that?"

"Usually." She started to walk away, then called back. "And wear that getup! People are sure to ask if you're in a play. We can use the publicity!" Then she did laugh, but it wasn't mean like it would be coming from Kimberly. It was more like, *Aren't we all cuckoo*, or something. I was beginning to think Drama Club might just be the place at Atwood Middle School where I belonged.

I searched through the costume room awhile longer, but I couldn't find a box of telephones, either. And since Amy didn't come back with a copy of the props list, there wasn't much else I could do in The Zone. Why not go outside, I thought, and paint flats with Ethan and Janette? I could learn more about that part of things. And maybe get another look at Jake.

Chapter Six

Ethan and I rode our bikes down to Donut Heaven Saturday afternoon. It was one of those great September days when you're perfectly comfortable in a sweatshirt, not too cold, not too warm.

The manager grumbled a little bit when we asked him about donating things for the play. "Everybody wants something for nothing," he said. But then he gave us some papers to fill out and said to let him know a week ahead of time exactly what we needed.

Just talking about doughnuts made us hungry for them. I had my allowance in my pocket, so we bought a box of day-old powdered-sugar doughnuts, our favorites, and stood by the bike rack snarfing them down. We'd each eaten two, and there were still two in the box.

"I don't want any more," Ethan said. "I'm thirsty now."

"I'll go get us some drinks. I've got money left."

Ethan was playing with the zipper on his sweatshirt. "We could go to my house and get drinks."

"We'll be dying by the time we ride all the way back," I said. "I'll get some orange juice at the Shop and

Save. It's cheaper there." He followed me across the parking lot to the supermarket. I handed him the doughnut box and went inside.

When I came out with the juice, Ethan had a funny look on his face.

"What's wrong?"

"I was just walking around and I went in back of the store, where the Dumpster is. There's somebody back there eating out of the trash!"

"The trash?"

We ran down to the end of the building, and I stuck my head around the side. Sure enough, there was an old woman, standing on a turned-over cardboard box, pulling stuff out of the Dumpster. She had some rotten-looking bananas sticking out of her pocket and a loaf of bread in her hand. She must have felt somebody watching her, because all of a sudden she turned around and glared at us.

It was Gracie, the old woman from the rummage sale. I jumped back so she couldn't see me. How could anybody eat old junk that had been thrown in the garbage?

"My mom knows her," I told Ethan. "She eats at the shelter sometimes. She's homeless."

Ethan screwed his face up like he does when you tell him bad news. "Really? Maybe we should give her these doughnuts."

I stared at him. "You mean, go up to her?"

"Why not? She won't hurt us or anything. Anyway, we don't want them, and she probably does."

I knew Ethan was right, but the idea of talking to the woman again made me shiver. She was so strange. "Why do we always have to do the right thing?" I whispered. "Just because my mother is a social worker twenty-four hours a day doesn't mean I have to be."

Ethan stared at me like I was speaking Martian. "She's *hungry*," he said. Ethan never argues; he just states his position and sticks to it. His mind was made up.

"Okay, okay," I said. "But you do the talking."

Ethan stared out into space for a minute and then sort of jumped around the corner. I followed more slowly. Gracie didn't take her eyes off us, but she got down from the box and backed away.

"Don't leave!" Ethan said. "We just want to give you these doughnuts. We ate all we want. You can have them." He held out the box to her.

For a minute we all just stood there, staring at one another. Then very slowly Gracie put out her hand and took the box. She opened it and stared at the two white doughnuts like they were made of gold. Then she picked them up with both hands, dropped the box on the ground, and started stuffing them into her mouth.

It wasn't too great watching her eat like that. When she was finished, there was white powder all over her face and on the front of her coat. She motioned to the quart of orange juice I'd forgotten I was holding in my hand.

"Oh!" I said. "We want this. I just bought it."

Gracie stood staring at the orange juice, and her arms dropped to her sides.

"Give it to her," Ethan whispered.

"But we didn't have any yet," I argued.

"We'll get some at my house."

I didn't have much choice. I stepped closer to the old woman and held out the carton.

As she took it from me, a smile wrinkled the corners of her mouth. "Good girl," she said. "Good boy." She opened the carton and poured the juice down her throat. It came out the corners of her mouth and ran down her neck in sticky rivers. I looked away, but Ethan seemed to be hypnotized by her.

When she finally stopped drinking, she leaned back against the Dumpster and smiled again. Even though her teeth were kind of yellow, it didn't seem like a crazy person's smile. She just seemed like a normal person saying, *Thank you*.

I started to move backward, figuring our good deed was done, but Ethan didn't budge. He motioned to the Dumpster. "You shouldn't eat that stuff out of there. It'll make you sick."

Gracie looked up at the metal bin like she'd just noticed it. She stood up very straight. "I'm the best cook in Rockingham County!" she announced. "Grace Jarvis Battle. No one makes a leg of lamb like Gracie."

Obviously she was a little bit scrambled. She kept

talking about herself like she was somebody else. "She's never been anybody's servant, Gracie hasn't. Never washed anybody's floor! Never scrubbed out a toilet that wasn't her own! No sirree. Not Gracie."

She carefully closed up the orange juice carton and hugged it to her chest like a teddy bear.

"Okay," I said. "We've got to go now." I pulled the back of Ethan's T-shirt to get him moving. I didn't feel like spending the whole day here. After all, I had my own life to think about, too.

But Gracie was wandering off, anyway, and we stopped again to listen. In a quiet, shaky voice, she was singing.

"Jesus loves me, this I know. For the Bible tells me so. Little ones to Him belong. They are weak, but He is strong." It made me shiver to listen.

Ethan joined in on the chorus. "Yes, Jesus loves me. Yes, Jesus loves me . . ."

I smacked him on the shoulder. "What are you doing? You want to follow her to the loony bin?"

"It's not loony. Don't you remember singing that song in Sunday school when you were little? I always liked it."

"Yeah, when I was five! But I don't sing it now, especially out in public!"

"We're not out in public. We're back by the Dumpster."

I sighed. Sometimes it's frustrating to have a friend who's so good-natured. "Oh, that makes it normal, then.

Come on. We're going to my house. I want to tell my mother about this!"

It took Ethan a minute to come out of his spell. I think he was humming as we rode home, but he stayed far enough behind me that I couldn't be sure. Three guesses what the song was.

By the time we got to my house, I'd forgotten I was even thirsty. I knew Mom and Dad were *both* home, for a change, and I figured I finally had a story that would make them listen to me. They were in the backyard, Mom cutting what was left of the grass, Dad pruning some forsythia bushes that were threatening to eat the patio furniture.

"Ethan!" Dad called out. "How've you been? Haven't seen you for a while!" As you can imagine, Ethan is the kind of friend parents love.

"I'm fine, Mr. Cunningham," Ethan said.

"Your dad fishing again today? We sure appreciated that trout he brought over last weekend."

"Yeah, he's at the lake again. You should go with him sometime."

"I'd love to. Soon as I get a free weekend. Soon as this yard shrivels up and dies."

"Don't blame the yard," Mom said. "You're just a workaholic."

"Takes one to know one," Dad shot back.

"Mom, guess who we saw?" I said, interrupting their bickering.

"Who?" She flopped down in a lawn chair, and our cat, Chesterfield leaped out of the bushes right into her arms. He knows people don't sit down much at our house, so he takes advantage of it anytime he finds a lap.

"That old woman Gracie from the shelter. She was eating out of the Dumpster behind the Shop and Save."

"Oh, no." Mom flopped her head back and stared at the sky.

"We gave her some doughnuts," Ethan assured her.

"And some orange juice," I added, as if it had been my idea.

She sighed. "Well, that was good of you. That poor woman. Of course I hear stories like this all the time, but I was hoping Gracie had someone watching out for her a little bit. I guess the world is short on guardian angels these days." She shook her head.

"She was *really* happy to get the food," I said, just to make sure she understood how superior Ethan and I were to the rest of the world.

"I'm sure she was, Bess," Mom said. "Thank you for helping her out."

I felt her smile hit me like a soft kiss, but instead of making me feel good, it just reminded me how much I'd missed that kind of stuff lately.

"If Gracie gets food at the shelter, why does she have to eat out of Dumpsters?" Ethan asked.

"The shelter only serves one meal a day. Would you guys be satisfied with one meal a day?"

Dad came over to join in the conversation. "On the weekends the lines get long. We can only serve the food we have. When the food runs out, the people at the end sometimes don't get anything except some of that bagged salad that's kind of brown around the edges. Maybe Gracie was at the end of the line."

The cordless phone sang out from the patio table. "That's probably my call," Mom said, reaching for it. She spoke briefly, then hung up. "Well, they'll be able to serve a lot of people tonight. That was Mr. Alexander calling from the country club. His daughter was married there today, and he asked me to take the leftover food to the shelter. Apparently there's quite a bit to pick up, everything from salmon steaks to wedding cake."

"Mmm. Sounds good," Dad said. "How about if I forget these silly bushes and go to the fish store for salmon steaks? I'll grill them with lemon and dill, the way you like them."

"Sounds great. Of course, as long as I don't have to cook, anything sounds great."

"It seems funny that we get to have fresh salmon steaks and they have to have somebody's leftovers," I said.

"It sure does," Mom said. "That's why I spend so much time at the shelter."

"What do you mean?"

"I don't want to forget that lots of people *aren't* eating fresh salmon steaks for dinner. It reminds me how fortunate I am. It also reminds me that fortunes can change, and that there's no shame in eating leftovers."

She pushed Chesterfield off her lap and dragged the mower back to the shed. "You know," she said when she came back, "you and Willy haven't been to the shelter in a long time. How about coming and helping out tomorrow?"

"Tomorrow?" Great. All I did was ask a few questions and now I was stuck volunteering. "Do I have to?"

"Yes, I think you do. At least once more."

"Could I come, too?" Ethan asked, his face all bright and shiny.

"Of course," Dad said, "as long as it's okay with your parents."

I gave Ethan my meanest look. If he was going, too, there was no chance I could get out of it.

"Ethan!" I said, once Mom and Dad had left on their separate errands. "What do you want to go to the shelter for?"

He shrugged. "To see it. To help other people like that old lady. It made me feel kind of good."

"But what if somebody sees us going in there?"

"Like who?"

"Like somebody from school. Like somebody we just met working on the play or something. What would they think?"

Ethan looked stumped. "I don't know. I guess they'd think we were volunteering at the shelter. What else *would* they think?"

"That we're weird hanging around all those crazy people. Or we're goody-goodies or something. Or maybe even that we *have* to eat there."

Ethan shook his head. "Bess, sometimes you think about things too much."

"Sometimes you don't think enough," I said. But there was nothing to do about it now. Mom had obviously made up her mind: We were going.

Chapter Seven

If you think I was mad, you should have seen Willy. He already had plans for Sunday, plans that involved a *girl*. So far in his life, Willy hadn't managed to involve many girls in his plans, so this was a big deal.

"How long do I have to hang out with the deviants?" he asked Mom.

"Use that word to describe people again," Mom said in her don't-push-me voice, "and you'll be hanging out in your own room for a week." Neither of us had any doubt she meant it.

"But, Mom," he whined, resorting to begging now, "I've wanted to ask Lauren out for weeks! Now I finally get up the nerve and I have to cancel it?"

"You'll be done at the shelter by two. You can go out then."

"We were going on a picnic! She was bringing food!"

"What were you bringing?" I asked. "Your pathetic excuse for a car?" The heap had been sitting in the drive-way with the hood up for days.

"Ask Lauren to come with us!" Mom said brightly. I

had just taken a drink of orange juice, and it snorted out my nose.

Willy kicked his backpack across the floor. "Right. Great idea, Mom," he said as he stomped out the back door.

So, after church on Sunday we changed clothes, picked up Ethan, who was so excited you'd think we were going to an amusement park, and headed downtown to the Derby Street Shelter. Willy had gotten his junker running, so he was following behind us.

Ethan leaned over the front seat to ask Mom and Dad all kinds of questions about how they first got involved with the shelter, while I slumped against the door, wishing it were all over already. I couldn't believe it. The only way I got to spend a day with my parents was to be an unpaid servant, like them. Why they got a bigger kick out of dinner at a homeless shelter than dinner at *our* home, I couldn't imagine.

Once you drive a block or so past the high school, everything starts to look run-down. Most of the stores that used to be there are shut now, and the windows are either broken or soaped up. A few stores are still open: a drugstore, a locksmith, an appliance place where the washing machines in the window look dusty. Some of the places don't even have signs, so you can't figure out what they sell.

The shelter didn't look so bad from the outside, not as bad as I remembered. A few years ago some high school kids painted a mural on the front. One of those scenes where all kinds of people, all races and colors, join together, some people singing, some building things, some eating, little kids running around. As if that's what it was like inside: a Perfect World. The painting was real colorful, though, and it did spruce up the building. There was a sign by the door that said DERBY STREET SHELTER in fancy letters, like it was a gift shop or something.

But to me it was like getting a present wrapped in beautiful paper and when you open it the stuff inside is old and broken. That's the way I remembered the shelter, and I wasn't anxious to walk through the front door again.

It was still early, so there were only volunteers inside, but some of them looked pretty scruffy, too. It seemed like everybody was wearing a sweatshirt and a straggly ponytail, men and women both. Mom looked like that, too, but Dad looked like a lawyer, even in jeans and a T-shirt. Everybody shouted hello to us.

"Hey, you brought the whole family, huh?" A black guy with a white apron, a gray beard, and a huge pair of clogs clomped over to us. "That's not Bess, your little baby, is it?" He was staring at me with amazement. The baby stared right back.

"I'm afraid it is," Mom said. "All grown up. And this is her friend Ethan. And you remember our son, Willy. They've come to help out today." Willy was already leaning against a wall in the corner looking about as helpful as a stray dog.

62

Mom continued the introductions. "Kids, this is Harold Wyman. He's in charge of the kitchen here."

"Yes I am, and I'm a happy man on the days your father comes in to help me cook. Those days I can sit back and everything runs smooth as a river without me paying it any attention."

Dad put one hand on Harold's back. "Actually Harold just lets me cook because I always bring a vat of my famous homemade hot sauce on chili days. Isn't that right?"

Harold laughed. "Well, that does influence me a little bit, Bill, I must admit."

Ha-ha. Harold didn't know what the rest of us went through the nights Dad decided he had to make more stupid hot sauce. Mom always managed to have a meeting to go to, but Willy and I usually just barricaded ourselves in the den with a pizza. The stink of that stuff goes right through walls. I don't know what's in it, but it makes your eyes water and your throat sore. Holding your nose is no help at all. I'd sooner eat nails.

"So, which of you wants to work in the kitchen, and which out front?" Mom asked.

"Kitchen!" I volunteered immediately. That way at least I wouldn't have to deal with all those people. What if that toothless guy showed up again?

"I'll work out front," Ethan said, the traitor.

"What about you, son?" Dad asked Willy. "Kitchen? Help us make spaghetti sauce for two hundred?"

63

"Whatever," Willy muttered. I couldn't see what he was so mad about. He'd arranged to pick up his new girlfriend at two thirty. Her gourmet sandwiches wouldn't get moldy that soon.

"Okay," Mr. Wyman said. "Kitchen help this way. Alice, you can show the boy there about setting up the steam table and putting out the fine silver. Later we've got to talk. We might be getting the price down on the place next door."

"Oh, that's great, Harold," Mom said. "Not a day too soon, either. Weather's getting cool already."

The kitchen wasn't really that bad. Dad and Harold—he told us to call him Harold right off—were like a comedy act or something. Together they made this huge cauldron of spaghetti sauce, pretending to put in things like eye of newt and alligator toenails while they were really adding garlic and oregano. Harold acted like he was putting in an old tennis ball, but then he made it disappear into thin air. It was nice to see Dad having such a good time. He seemed more relaxed than he usually did at home, where he's always looking at his watch to see if he's got time to finish one thing before he goes to the next.

Willy and I got the job of washing and ripping up about a hundred heads of lettuce for the salad table. Lots of other people came in, too, and they all seemed to know one another. It was actually starting to look kind of like the mural on the front of the building.

"This isn't as bad as I remember," I told Willy.

"That's because we aren't out front. Wait till your friend Ethan gets a load of the clientele." Willy shivered.

"They aren't that bad. They're just people who can't afford food," I said, trying to convince myself. Also, I didn't like to agree with Willy if I could help it.

"That's not what you thought a few years ago when that guy wanted you to dig through the garbage for his molars." Willy laughed.

"That was different. I was a little kid then."

"Oh, right. I forgot how grown-up you are now. Miss Middle School."

I hated that Willy was so much older than me that my life was just a faraway joke to him. Mom told me once that as we got older, five years wouldn't seem like such a big difference, but she was probably just saying that. It seemed that for every year older I got, Willy got two. I mean, when he was nine and I was four, he'd at least pull me in the wagon sometimes; now he acted like I was too childish to be allowed in the backseat of his car.

As we finished chopping the carrots and peppers, I could hear people starting to line up outside at the door.

"Gather round for a minute, please, folks," Harold sang out. "Make a circle." Most people had been here before, so we just did what they did, joined hands and stood in a circle, looking at Harold. I was right between a young couple who spoke Spanish to each other over my head. I asked if they wanted to stand together, but the girl said, "Oh, no, you stay!" and gave me a big smile.

Willy had to hold Dad's hand on one side and some middle-aged woman's on the other, and I could tell he wasn't too happy about it. I mean, Willy probably hadn't held hands with anybody since kindergarten. I was pretty sure he was thinking this circle thing was too sappy for words.

"As you can hear, our guests have arrived," Harold said. "I hope no one will forget that these folks *are* our guests. Please greet them with a smile, as you would a guest in your own home, for the welcome we give here at Derby Street is as important to them as the warm food in their stomachs." I thought that was a nice way to put it, although I guessed that if they had to choose, they'd take the food over the smile.

Then we all looked at our shoes while Harold said a prayer. At the end of the prayer, he clapped his hands and said, "Open the doors and go to work!"

"Run the salad stuff out to the table, would you, Bess?" Dad called out. "Willy, you can slice the bread."

Willy smirked as I picked up the big silver container and backed through the door. There they were, our guests, starting through the line, kind of tired-looking, but not really scary at all. Some of them were quiet and kept to themselves, choosing tables in the corners, while others yelled hello to their friends and sat in groups. There were a few people who were dressed really raggedy or in too many layers, and seemed to be having conversations with themselves. But mostly it wasn't that different from the cafeteria at school, just people meeting and eating and talking, then going on their way.

Mom was second on the serving line. A woman named Dorrie put the spaghetti on the plate, and Mom poured the sauce over it. Then she held the plate out while Ethan plopped a roll on it and handed it to the person waiting. Of course, she knew a lot of people by name, and they knew her. As I stood watching, I felt really proud of my mom, not just for working on the line, but for enjoying it so much.

Ethan was having a good time, too. I could tell. Mom was introducing him to the people she knew the best, and they were all telling him, "Thank you very much, young man," and things like that. He was all red in the face and smiling.

"Hey, Kitchen Help!" Harold shouted from the doorway. "We gotta clean up this mess and get ready for the dirty dishes!" They sure worked you hard.

Pretty soon the place was really noisy. There were people bringing their trays to the clearing table, and other people getting another cup of coffee and sitting around talking, and one table full of people singing some kind of hymns back in the corner. And kids. That surprised me. I hadn't remembered the kids, but today there were about a dozen little kids running around, playing, just like kids do anywhere.

The kitchen people were laughing, too, while they

banged carts of dirty dishes around and washed everything up. Somebody brought a radio and had it tuned to a jazz station and turned up loud. Some people even danced a little while they worked. It was kind of cool.

Willy and I got assigned to the clearing table, where people brought their trays when they were finished. A few people forgot to clear their own tables, so when things got quieter, I went around to get the dishes.

I was dumping a couple of trays into the trash when all of a sudden I felt my new glasses starting to slip down my nose. I had trays in both hands and even though I tried to keep the glasses in place by screwing up my nose, they slipped down, anyway, right into the trash!

"My glasses!" I yelled.

Willy saw the whole thing and laughed so hard, he just about wet his pants.

"Yuck!" I said, peering into the soggy mass of spaghetti, salad, and used napkins.

"Lemme reach in there and get 'em out for you, child." Before I could say anything, a small black man leaned over the barrel and picked through the slop. In just a second he'd pulled my glasses out. "Here you go. They needs some washin'," he said, handing them to me. "I imagine I do, too!" He laughed.

"Thank you. You didn't have to—," I said.

"Nothin' to it, dear." He gave me a big smile that was full of holes. "Newly Puckett at your service." He bowed at the waist and then walked off.

The whole thing was so weird. I gave Willy a hard shove as I went into the kitchen to wash my glasses. He was laughing so much, he couldn't stand up straight.

There were still some trays to clear and, anyway, I couldn't stand listening to Willy, who was just *making* himself laugh now, so I went back out into the main room. An old woman was sitting by herself at a back table, but it looked like she was finished eating. There were two trays on her table, so I went back to get them.

I'd been trying to smile at people, like Harold said to, so when I got to the table, I gave the woman a big grin and she looked right up at me. It was Gracie. "Oh!" I said. "Hello."

She looked a little scared, like the day we found her by the Dumpster, but she smiled. "Good girl," she said.

I wasn't sure if she remembered me or if she just called everybody "good girl." "Do you know who I am?" I asked her.

"Good girl," she said again.

"Hey," Willy called to me from the kitchen door. "We're not finished in here."

"It's okay, Willy," Mom said. "You can take off now if you want. Thank you."

Willy looked a little embarrassed as he took off his apron and sauntered out the door, like he was in no big hurry to get going, but he would if he wasn't needed anymore.

Gracie had finished her dinner and was hugging a

69

cup of coffee in her hands as if it were a cold day. She was still wearing several layers of clothes and she smelled a little musty, but not too bad.

"Do you want more coffee?" I asked her.

"Gracie likes coffee," she said, and held out her cup. I went to the pot and got her a refill, then sat down across from her. For one thing, I was exhausted from running around here half the day, but I also kind of wanted to talk to her. It was funny—recognizing her in this place, where I didn't know anybody, made her seem almost like a friend, except, of course, I didn't really know her, either. She didn't seem all that crazy sitting here drinking coffee—definitely strange, but not totally nuts or anything.

"My name is Bess," I said. "And you're Gracie?"

"Gracie." She looked shy at first, but then she sat up straight in her chair. "Grace Jarvis Battle. My husband was Ernest Warren Battle."

"My name is Bess Cunningham. My parents work here every other Sunday. Are you from Atwood? Did you grow up here?" What I really wanted to know was, how did you end up here, at the Derby Street Shelter, eating leftovers, but I couldn't ask that.

She shook her head. "Born in Linton. Moved to Atwood with Ernest. He was born round here." Suddenly her voice got louder. "I was married thirty-five years. He was a good man, Ernest was. It was not his fault about the business. When he died, there was nothing left. Nothing left." She shook her head.

"Do you have any children?" I wasn't sure if I was being too nosy or not, but Gracie didn't seem to mind.

"No, never had any. Wish I had. Wish I had. Only a sister. Dead now, too." Her face wrinkled up all of a sudden, like the ground after an earthquake. She spoke loudly again. "That girl's no good. Evil and hateful. She could help me, but she won't! Rich people are like that. They spit on you."

"Who won't help you? Your niece? My mother said you had a niece."

But Gracie wasn't paying any attention to me anymore. "I didn't spill the coffee that time. No sirree. Sometimes they spit on me. I don't like that, no sirree." Her face was twitching now. "It's not my fault. It's not Ernest's fault."

Obviously she was a little crazy, but still, how could her niece let her sleep out on the street and eat out of Dumpsters?

"Where does your niece live?"

She'd settled down a little bit, and she smiled at me again. "I can have two cups of coffee if I want to. Yes sirree. I can even have three cups if I want." She sounded just like a little kid, and it made me smile.

Chapter Eight

The set crew was working every day after school, so I worked with them. I told Suzanne how much fun it was down in The Zone, and she and her friend Anna started coming, too. We painted, we sanded, we nailed, we crawled around on the floor of The Zone in search of items Amy just *knew* were there somewhere. It was great. And just as I'd predicted, Ethan and I were getting to know a lot of new kids.

The one I was most interested in getting to know was Jake, but, of course, he was the impossible one. He didn't really have conversations with people; he mostly just ordered them around. Normally I wouldn't even care about a person who acted so snotty, but there was just something about the way he stood there with his hands in his back pockets. It's hard to explain.

And then there was the problem of my new wardrobe. I'd decided to forget about the hat after the day it was turned into a hallway Frisbee, but that wasn't the only problem. One afternoon while we were painting some platforms outside, I tossed my scarf over my shoulder, not realizing that Jake was standing behind me, and it hit him in the face. He looked at me in this disgusted way and said, "Your clothes are more trouble than you're worth, Cunningham."

That really hurt my feelings, but I tried to act like it was just a joke. "I can't help it if you don't look where you're going!" He didn't bother to reply.

Then, about fifteen minutes later, I was getting up from kneeling on the ground, where I'd been painting one of the platforms, and I accidentally stepped on the hem of my skirt, which made me fall forward. Well, you know how if you're falling, you grab whatever is nearby to try to hold yourself up? Turns out what was nearby was Jake, and instead of just holding on, I must have sort of pushed him, and he fell forward onto the platform we'd just painted. Grass green paint all over his jeans, his shirt, his arms, his hands, and even a little spot on his chin. He was not amused.

"Damn it!" he said as he stood up and inspected the damage.

"I'm sorry! It's washable paint, isn't it?" I said. "I didn't mean to."

"You never mean to! Listen, a stage manager can't be getting in everybody's way all the time! Your clothes are a hazard. Either wear regular stuff from now on, or stay away from me!"

I pretended to be mad, too, and stalked inside to wash out my brush at the sink. I wanted to get away from the others just in case I started to cry, which seemed like a good possibility unless I could swallow it back quickly. It's not like he had no reason to be mad, but still, he didn't have to be so mean about it. I'd tried to be cool and funny and joke with him, but he never did anything but bark at me. Only a couple of tears actually squeezed out, but it made me feel a little better.

The truth was, I was pretty sick of the skirts and scarves myself. I'd gotten paint all over the skirts and tripped on the hems more times than I liked to admit. And the scarves just plain got in the way. But I needed *something* to set me apart, didn't I? Something to make Jake notice me.

On the other hand, I figured it might be wise to be invisible around Jake for a while. Maybe once he stopped being mad at me, he'd learn to appreciate my good qualities, whatever those might be. I decided I'd keep wearing my big shirts, but I'd go back to my jeans, and once they got some paint on them, I'd at least look a little bit different. And when the play was over, I could go back to my outfits if I wanted to.

By the next week Ms. Plumbly told me to be at rehearsals with her so I could start getting the whole play in my mind. I hated leaving The Zone, and Ethan and Amy and Jake, but Ms. Plumbly assured me that in a few more weeks, when the actors knew what they were doing, stage and backstage would come together, and the play would be "on its feet."

Ms. Plumbly explained that she liked her stage manager to be more like an assistant director. I was supposed to follow her around like a golden retriever and remember everything she said that was important. And since I couldn't always tell right away what was important and what wasn't, I took lots of notes.

Of course, Kimberly Pringle was a huge pain in the rear end, always putting in her two cents' worth, which nobody cared about.

"Ms. Plumbly, don't you think Ursula should really be standing in front of the other girls in the group in this scene? I mean, Ursula is really a more important character than the others. She gets to talk!"

"Don't worry, Kimberly," Ms. Plumbly said. "Everyone will know how important Ursula is even if she's not standing at center stage."

"Will Ursula's costume be just a little bit different? So she stands out from the rest?" Kimberly asked sweetly. The other girls were really starting to get ticked off, I could tell.

"The costume committee will make those decisions next week, Kimberly. Let's just learn the lines for now, shall we?" Ms. Plumbly had to spend a lot of time just getting Kimberly to shut up so they could keep rehearsing.

When Mom picked Ethan and me up at five o'clock on Friday, my head was spinning. Where Birdie should stand, how twenty-eight other people should move across the stage, who should pull at Birdie's scarf, who faints when, and who'd better catch the mayor's wife if he knows what's good for him. And that was just one scene.

Mom listened to my problems, then said, "I've had quite a day myself. After school I went with Harold to confront Mr. Atchison, the owner of the building we want for the women's shelter. His price was still much too high, and we knew there must be something odd going on."

"What was the problem?"

Mom sighed. "Seems the price would go down significantly for anyone else who wanted to buy the property. He just doesn't want the shelter to take it over. He says the reason the property values are so low now is because the Derby Street Shelter attracts so many 'undesirables.' That was his word. I tried to tell him the shelter is just a response to the problems that were already in the downtown area, but he wouldn't listen."

"So what will you do?" I said. "You can't give up!"

Mom smiled. "Of course not. Harold saved the day. He kept this very understanding look on his face the whole time he was sweet-talking the guy, and towered over him a little bit, too. and by the time we left, Mr. Atchison had agreed to come down to the kitchen Sunday morning to see what really goes on."

"That's great!" Ethan said. "Can we come with you again?"

"It's fine with me."

"But, Mom," I said, not so sure about all this, "what if he comes down and gets grossed out or something? What if he really *does* think they're all horrible?"

"Did you think they were all horrible when you were there?"

I thought of the men standing patiently, waiting for Mom to hand them their plates. The families with their little kids running around. The table full of women, whose legs had bug bites on them, who probably didn't have a place to sleep at night. The hymn singers. Newly Puckett. Gracie.

"No," I said. "Actually I was kind of surprised. They mostly seemed like regular people. Some of them were a little strange, but not in a scary way."

"I hope that's what Mr. Atchison will think, too," Mom said.

"We'll show him," Ethan said. "The shelter is a great place!"

I had to admit I was a little excited about it myself. Maybe we could help convince him somehow. Of course, I *had* planned to use Sunday to memorize all the entrances and exits in *Bye Bye Birdie*, which was also important.

But once you'd actually been to the shelter, and seen Gracie and talked to Newly, you couldn't just forget about it. It wasn't a play or a game. It was real, maybe more real than anything else in your life.

Chapter Nine

When I showed up at Ethan's house the next morning, I could hear what was going on inside before I even got off my bike. The littlest girls were having meltdowns.

Ethan's mom had the baby in the high chair and was trying to get a few spoonfuls of cereal into her mouth, but Jenny, who's five, was jumping up and down and pulling on her other arm, which threw off Mrs. Riley's aim. As I came in the door, a teaspoonful of warm glop hit Susie in the nose, and she shrieked that shriek that makes you want to put your hands over your ears. Then she took her fingers and pushed the oatmeal farther up inside her nostrils.

Mrs. Riley always stayed calm, but sometimes I wondered if that was because she was too tired to get upset. "Jenny," she said, "we'll go for a walk as soon as I feed your sister."

"Now!" Jenny insisted. "And I get to ride in the stroller."

"Susie rides in the stroller. You know that."

"I do!" Another scream that could puncture your eardrums.

"Hello, Bess," Mrs. Riley said. "Ethan's in the living room talking to his father. Go on in."

On my way out of the kitchen I passed Amanda, Ethan's older sister, who doesn't acknowledge my existence now that she's in high school. She had a problem for Mrs. Riley to solve, too. "Mom, Caroline wore my good silk blouse, and now it's all wrinkled and I wanted to wear it today!" Caroline is Ethan's oldest sister, just a year older than Amanda, and the two of them are always arguing about something.

"Well, you know where the iron is, Amanda," Mrs. Riley said.

"Could *you* do it, Mom? It's not fair that I have to. I told her she couldn't wear it! And besides, I'm writing a paper for my biology class."

Mrs. Riley sighed. "You'll have to wait if you want me to do it."

Amanda brightened right up. "That's okay! As long as it's ready by noon. Thanks, Mom." She skipped back upstairs.

I was always amazed by scenes like this at the Rileys' house—it was like visiting a foreign country or something. On the one hand I felt sorry for Mrs. Riley, who seemed like she had to do everything for everybody, but then again, I thought it must be kind of nice to have a mother who's always around when you need her help.

Ethan was pacing around the living room while his dad sat in one of those big recliner chairs that take up half the room. He had the newspaper on his lap, and his hair was standing up funny, like he hadn't combed it yet.

"Bess! Tell my dad the shelter is okay. It's not a dangerous place or anything."

Mr. Riley nodded at me. "Ethan says he wants to go with your family to this shelter place again tomorrow. But I don't know if that's such a good idea."

"Why not?" Ethan yelled.

"Calm down, Ethan. I'm just trying to look out for you. That place is in a bad area of town. I didn't realize the last time exactly where you were going."

"My parents go there all the time, Mr. Riley. Nothing bad has ever happened to them," I pointed out.

"There's always a first time," Mr. Riley said. That didn't seem like a very nice thing to say, but then I had an idea— the same one Harold had used on Mr. Atchison, the owner of the building next door to the shelter.

"Mr. Riley, why don't you come, too? Then you'd see that it's not dangerous. And the shelter can always use more volunteers."

"Yeah, Dad!" Ethan said. "You should come, too!"

Mr. Riley frowned. "Well, Bess . . . you see . . . I don't think I could . . . Ethan, you know I'm very busy on the weekends."

He sure didn't look very busy. It was Mrs. Riley who looked like she didn't have a spare minute. Just as I thought that, she appeared in the doorway. "Tell you what, Daniel, you stay here with the girls tomorrow and

I'll go to the shelter with Ethan. I'd like to help out."

I could tell Mr. Riley had some things he wanted to say, but he wouldn't say them in front of me. He just muttered, "Well, I suppose I could . . . if you think that's a good idea. . . ." Then he stormed off outside.

"If he wants to go fishing again, he can just take the girls with him," Mrs. Riley said with a little laugh. "Serving food to people other than my own family for a change will seem like a holiday to me."

Ethan's bike was on his front porch. "Let's get out of here before Dad blows a gasket. Where should we go?"

"The supermarket. I brought some money to get food for Gracie," I said. "So she doesn't have to eat that junk from the trash."

Ethan looked embarrassed. "I spent my allowance on school lunches. I don't have anything left."

"That's okay. I took money from the Emergency Jar. Mom won't care."

Actually, I didn't think she'd even notice. The Emergency Jar is just an old rinsed-out mayonnaise jar we keep in the back of a kitchen cabinet. Every week Mom puts a certain amount of money in it. Most of it's lunch money for me and Willy so we don't bug her every morning before she's fully awake and functioning. But we can take money out for other things, too: not for clothes or CDs or things like that, but for anything we think is an emergency, things that can't wait until they get home—since they're gone so much with work and meetings. We're on our honor, Mom says, not to abuse the privilege, and we usually don't, although Willy has been in negotiations with her lately about whether or not auto parts should be considered an emergency.

Mom was still asleep when I left today, so I decided Gracie definitely qualified as an emergency, especially if I didn't get around to mentioning it to anyone.

"I only have until noon," Ethan said as we turned off Hillside Avenue onto Mt. Vernon Street.

"How come?"

"The play. We have to finish painting the flats today."

"You do? Is Janette going?"

"I think so, if she can escape from her mother after her voice lesson. You know, she skipped her swimming lesson Monday. I think she might be starting to stand up to her mother a little bit more. Yesterday Jake told her she was doing a really good job."

I felt a small firecracker explode in my chest. "Will Jake be there today?"

"Sure. He's always there."

"Do you think I could come, too? The cast isn't rehearsing, and I like to paint sets."

"I don't see why not. Jake's always trying to get more people to show up."

Jake, Jake, Jake. I hadn't seen much of him since I'd started working in the theater with Ms. Plumbly. But I'd certainly thought about him. I don't know why he seemed so much more interesting to me than any other guys, but he did. At night before I went to sleep I'd make up little scenes in which we'd run into each other someplace, and he'd be so happy to see me again, and he'd say he'd missed me, and I'd make a clever, witty remark that I could never actually think of if he was standing in front of me, and then we'd . . . well, you know what I mean. It's embarrassing to admit, and I would *never* tell Ethan, who doesn't think about stuff like this at all, as far as I know. He'd think I was nuts. Maybe I'd tell Janette sometime, though.

We rode our bikes right around back to the Dumpster, but Gracie was nowhere in sight.

"She'll show up," Ethan said. "Let's go buy the stuff."

Sure enough, by the time we came back out with a loaf of bread, some apples, and cheese and orange juice, there she was, dragging a garbage bag and heading for the Dumpster.

"Gracie!" I yelled as we ran after her.

I guess we were so anxious, we scared her a little. She tried to run away when she saw us coming.

"Wait!" I said. "It's us. Good girl! Good boy!"

She turned around and gave us a hard look, then smiled. "Good girl. Good boy. Don't hurt Gracie."

The way she looked at us, kind of softly, I realized with a shock that she must have been pretty once. It was still there in a few places—her gray blue eyes that sparkled in the sun, the way her thin fingers brushed her hair back out of her face, her almost-shy smile. I tried to imagine her younger, in a clean dress, married to old Ernest Warren Battle. I wished I had a better imagination.

We handed over the food we'd just bought, and she sat right there beside the Dumpster and wolfed it down. While she ate, we tried to talk to her, but she couldn't answer too well with her mouth crammed full.

"My name is Ethan, and this is Bess," Ethan said. Gracie looked up, but kept eating.

"And you're Gracie," he continued. She nodded.

"Grace Jarvis Battle," I said, and she smiled, which was gross since her mouth was so full.

I waited until she swallowed that bite. "Where do you sleep at night, Gracie?" I asked her. It was the question that kept following me around, especially at night as I lay in bed on my soft sheets, covered with a warm blanket.

She looked at me closely and then turned around to point in the direction of the stores across the street.

"The shopping center?"

She nodded.

"Where? In the back?" I didn't think the police would let people sleep right out in front of the stores.

She nodded again. "Montoni's Furniture," she whispered. "They have a loading dock in back. Up high. When it rains, I don't get too wet. No sirree." She smiled.

"Don't you get cold at night?" Ethan asked, and we both shivered a little just thinking about sleeping outside in the rain in October.

She took another bite of bread and chewed it awhile. Then she said, "Somebody stole my blanket. Had to leave it behind the store in the daytime. Too heavy. Now it's gone."

84

Ethan and I just looked at each other. We didn't know what to say. It was too depressing thinking of Gracie sleeping on Montoni's loading dock without even a blanket.

"Probably the manager," she said. "He hates me, too." She didn't say it like she was angry, though. She just said it.

We couldn't stay much longer. We wanted to grab some lunch before we headed over to the school. Although it does kind of kill your appetite to hang out by the Dumpster with Gracie.

Just then the back door of the market opened, and the manager walked out with one of the stock boys, who was dragging two bags full of plastic bottles.

"The recycle stuff goes in the far bin," he was telling him. "Make sure you don't mix up the brands." He turned around then and noticed us. "What's going on here? Get out of there!" He came running at us the way my dad chases the neighbors' dog out of his tomato garden, his arms flying around his head.

Gracie jumped up and stuffed the rest of the cheese and two apples in her big coat pockets.

"We weren't doing anything," I said. "We bought some food in the store for Gracie."

"I've got eyes! You were digging through my Dumpster, making a big mess out here. I've seen this old bag here before." He glared at Gracie, and she started backing away.

"Really, we just—," Ethan started to explain again.

"I don't need any lip from you kids! Beat it now or I'll call the police!" Gracie started to run when he said that. Ethan and I weren't real crazy about the idea, either, so we backed off, too.

"Some people just don't have enough to eat!" I yelled back at the guy, thinking maybe I could still make him understand.

"Yeah, yeah, some people ought to get a job! Jeez, bratty kids and cracked old ladies—what next?" He slammed back inside the building.

For a minute Ethan and I just stood there looking at the door he'd disappeared through. How could he say things like that? He didn't even *know* Gracie. By the time we started looking around for her, she was gone, too, probably dragging her bag along the Dumpster trail in back of the shopping center. We rode our bikes home without saying a word to each other. Sometimes it's too hard to think about things out loud.

While Janette and I were painting signs that said, CONRAD BIRDIE FAN CLUB, which the girls were supposed to carry around onstage, I told her about Gracie.

"I can't believe your mother lets you do things like that," Janette said.

"Like what?"

"Like hanging around the supermarket with bag ladies. My mother would have a fit."

"Your mother always has a fit," I said. Janette made a face, but she didn't disagree. It's no wonder Janette is so nervous, the way her mother worries about every little thing she does. I guess the upside of having a mother who's too busy to notice you is pretty much the same as the downside: She's too busy to notice you.

I looked up and saw Ethan running toward us. He and some other boys had been lugging flats in and out of The Zone Annex, the shed at the edge of the parking lot, under Amy's command. "Bess!" he was yelling as he slid to a stop in front of us. "I've got it!"

"Got what?"

"A place for Gracie to stay. It's inside, and nobody will notice. If we can get her a few blankets, it'll be pretty warm, I think. At least for a while."

"Ethan, be quiet!" I said. "You want everybody to hear you?"

He looked around. "Nobody's listening. Nobody even cares." He looked at Janette. "Do you care?"

She shrugged. "You two always have some weird scheme. It doesn't bother me, unless you expect me to be part of it."

"I just don't think we should advertise this," I said.

"Fine. I won't tell you my idea, then." He turned around as if he was going to walk away.

"Oh, right. Like you'd ever be mad at me for more than thirty seconds," I said. "Tell me, Ethan, just don't yell it."

He stooped down to be close to us. "The Zone

Annex," he said, smiling proudly. "Is that a great idea or what? There's plenty of room in it now. We're taking the biggest flats up onstage today."

I wasn't sure. "Isn't there a lock on it?"

Ethan grinned. "It's broken. I didn't notice it myself—nobody would—but Jake mentioned it. He said he's been trying to get the custodian to fix it all year but the guy never gets around to it. So Jake just makes it look like the lock is closed, hoping nobody pulls on it to check."

I put my hands on Ethan's shoulders. "I think you just might be a genius!"

Janette stood up, chewing on her nails. "You guys are going to be in *so much* trouble," she said.

"We are not," I said.

"If anybody finds out, you will be," she said.

"If anybody finds out, we'll know you told," I said. Which was sort of mean, because I knew Janette was way too wimpy to tell on us.

"Me? I won't tell! You know I won't!"

Ethan and I continued plotting. "The flats won't have to go back in there until Thanksgiving week," I said. "By then, maybe the women's shelter will be ready to open."

"And if it isn't, we'll come up with something else," Ethan said confidently.

"We'll bring her down here tomorrow, after lunch at the shelter," I said. Ethan and I gave each other a couple of high fives while Janette shook her head and looked the other way.

Chapter Ten

Of course Janette hadn't ridden her bike to school, because bike riding was way too dangerous if you were planning on being a dancer. Not that Janette was planning on that, but her mother still had hopes. Ethan and I offered to wait out front with her until her mom came to pick her up, because we knew she hated waiting all alone—it makes her too visible. But something funny was going on.

"Really, you guys don't have to wait," she kept saying. "Go on home. My mom will be here in a few minutes." That just wasn't like Janette.

Jake walked by as we were discussing it, and I'd swear he winked at us. At me, I guess, or maybe at Janette, although that didn't make any sense. He'd hardly spoken to me all afternoon, except to say, "I see you're not wearing your dress-up clothes today." Before I could come up with a clever response, he was halfway across the lawn already. Could he really have winked at me? Why? What did it mean? Was I ever going to be able to have an actual conversation with him?

By the time Ethan and I had ridden our bikes home,

our plan to help Gracie was beginning to take shape. Unfortunately it seemed that it would be necessary to include a third partner, my brother, Willy. Convincing him to help us was going to take an ingenious strategy, which, at the moment, we didn't have.

The thing was, our parents weren't going to let us leave the shelter to go walking around with Gracie in downtown Atwood. We'd need a car and a driver, and that meant Willy.

He was in the driveway when we got back, his head stuck down into the guts of that ancient vehicle, as usual. Which meant he was probably not in a good mood.

"Working on your car?" I asked as sweetly as possible.

Willy straightened up and glared at me. "No, I'm grilling hamburgers."

"Sure wish I could help you," Ethan said, peering at the engine. "It looks pretty complicated."

"Not for Willy," I said. "He know *all* about cars."

Willy gave us the eye. "Okay. What's going on?"

So we just told him. We needed him to go to the shelter with us tomorrow, drive his car, offer to give us a ride home, then drop Gracie off at the middle school on the way back. We tried to act like this was a pretty normal request.

Willy's mouth was standing open. "You two are out of your minds. You expect me to spend another Sunday at that shelter, drive you goons and some smelly, old bag lady around in my car, and then lie to Mom and Dad on top of it?"

"Oh, like you *never* lie to Mom and Dad," I said.

"Not about something *this* stupid."

"Please, Willy!" I begged. "It's the only way we can get her to the middle school!" I tried to work up a few tears, but I'm not very good at that kind of thing.

"Just tell Mom about it. She'll probably drive you there herself. That stuff is right up her alley."

"We thought about that," I said. "But we can't tell her—she works for the school district. She'd get in trouble if she helped somebody hide out on school property."

"Like you *won't* get in trouble!" he said. "You come up with the nuttiest ideas, Bess. You know I hate that shelter."

"It's not that bad. Listen, Willy, Ethan and I will do anything for you, *anything*." I hadn't actually cleared that with Ethan, but I figured we were desperate.

Willy kept banging around on his car, but I could tell he was thinking it over. Finally he said, "It would have to be *major* to make up for this."

"Name it," I said, thinking I would surely live to regret this promise.

He leaned back against the car and looked up at the clouds, trying to think up something impossible. "Okay. If you can get me a date with Ethan's sister Caroline, I'll do it."

"What? I thought you already had a girlfriend," I said.

"We broke up." I could tell by the way he said it, breaking up probably wasn't *his* idea.

"You want to go out with my *sister*?" Ethan said. He looked sort of scared, as if Willy were contemplating a date with the Bride of Frankenstein.

"You know Caroline. You can ask her yourself," I said.

Willy's face got red. "That's the deal. Get me a date with Caroline, and I'll drive you. Otherwise, forget it."

The thing is, Willy talks big, but he's really pretty shy, especially with girls. Caroline is a year younger than Willy, and she's Ethan's prettiest, most popular sister. She and Willy used to play together sometimes when they were little, but they haven't had much to do with each other for years. (That will never happen to me and Ethan—we are friends forever!) I know Willy has always kind of liked Caroline, but he never had the nerve to ask her out. He probably figured if we didn't pull it off, she'd just think it was some goofy prank Ethan and I had come up with.

So we headed straight over to Ethan's house. Caroline was in her room, staring into the mirror and messing with her hair. Ethan says she thinks she looks like Nicole Kidman, which is not as far-fetched as you might think.

"Whata you guys want?" Caroline was usually nicer to us than Amanda, but still not too happy to have mere children invading her teenage space.

"What do you think of my brother?" I began.

"Willy? He's okay. Kind of cute," she said.

That was a good beginning. "Ethan says you aren't going with anybody right now."

"Thanks, Ethan. Blab it to everybody."

"It's not a big secret," Ethan said. I jabbed him with my elbow. We couldn't afford to make her angry.

"Anyway," I continued. "If Willy asked you out, would you go out with him?"

"He wouldn't ask me out," Caroline said. "He never even talks to me."

"*If* he did," Ethan said, exasperated.

Caroline bent over the mirror and looked deeply into her own eyes. "Willy thinks I'm still the little kid across the street or something."

"I happen to know he likes you," I said, thinking if Willy ever found out I'd told her that, he'd shove me in the dryer and set it on permanent press.

"He does?" She looked at me, surprised, then curled a lock of hair around her finger. "Well, I might go out with him, if he asked me."

"We have to know *for sure,*" Ethan said.

"Why do you care so much?" Caroline was getting suspicious.

"We're just curious," I said. "I mean, because you live next door and all. And it seemed to us like you'd be a good couple." What did we know about good couples? We wouldn't even be twelve until next spring!

"Well, if Willy called me, I probably would go out with him."

"I think he's thinking about it," I said.

"So tell us definitely," Ethan insisted.

Caroline sighed. "What is with you? Okay. If he asked me, I'd definitely go out with him. Are you happy now?"

"Thank you!" I yelled as we ran down the stairs and out the front door.

"She'll go," I said, panting, as we pulled up in front of Willy. "All you have to do is call her, and she'll go out with you."

"She will?" His eyes floated up to a second-floor window in Ethan's house. "You were supposed to set the whole thing up," he said.

"Willy, doesn't it seem kind of dorky to have your little sister setting up your dates? We asked her and she said she'd go out with you if you called her."

"She said definitely," Ethan added.

"She did? Definitely?"

"All you have to do is call and set it up. Okay? Is that our part of the deal?" I asked him.

He hesitated and looked back at the lighted window. "I guess so. But I'm calling her right away to make sure before I turn my car into the Senior Citizen Welcome Wagon."

So he called her, and she probably giggled or something, and they made a date for Sunday night. Willy had a debt to pay.

He was in such a good mood the next day, thinking about his upcoming date, I was afraid Mom and Dad would suspect something. First of all, he announced breezily that he was coming to the shelter with us, then he offered to drive "the kids" in his car so Mom and Dad and Mrs. Riley wouldn't be all squashed together. Mom and Dad were so pleased at his sudden cooperativeness, they weren't even suspicious.

Dad clapped Willy on the shoulder. "Son, I'm proud of you for making this decision. It means a lot to me." Mom just stood there grinning. Willy looked slightly embarrassed by all the pride, but he didn't say anything.

"Mom, can I work out front today?" I asked when we got to the shelter.

"Sure! Why don't you and Ethan bring the trays around and start stacking the salad bowls on the table? Harold and I are going next door to meet Mr. Atchison and bring him over."

There was plenty to do to keep us all busy, which was good because I was starting to worry. What if Gracie didn't show up today? What if Mr. Atchison thought Derby Street was an awful place and decided he'd never sell his building for a women's shelter? For some reason I thought of how my Gramma Cunningham, before she died, always used to say, "Everything works out for the best." It made me feel safe as a little kid. But all you had to do was look around the Derby Street Shelter to see that things had not always worked out for the best for these people.

Mom and Harold had nervous looks on their faces

when they brought Mr. Atchison in. He had his arms folded across his chest like he was protecting his heart or something. Or maybe he didn't want to get his hands dirty.

Mom introduced him to everybody out front and then took him into the kitchen.

Harold sighed and plopped into a chair. "Glad to see you two back again. I guess you had so much fun last time, you couldn't stay away." He had a big grin now.

"I like this place," Ethan announced simply.

"It likes you, too, son," Harold said.

"So you think Mr. Atchison will like it?" I asked.

Harold shook his head. "Who knows? The man's hard to figure out. Your mother's plan is to stick him with your daddy for a while. So maybe he'll be impressed we got a big-shot lawyer making fried chicken in the kitchen." Harold laughed. "Who knows?"

"We should introduce him to Gracie," I said. "How could he let her sleep outside at night if he could change it?"

"I don't know, Bess. Maybe you're right. Maybe we just got to locate the man's heart," Harold said.

"But are we absolutely sure he's got one?" Mom said with a sigh, coming up to us. "He's so jumpy—you'd think we just led him onto Normandy Beach on D day."

"What's that?" I asked.

"A battle in World War II where lots of people died," Ethan explained. He knows that kind of stuff.

96

"Did you ever meet Gracie's niece?" I asked Harold. "The one who's so mean and won't take care of her?"

"She doesn't have a niece. She hasn't got any living relatives. We'da found one by now if she did."

"But Harold," Mom said, "Gracie told me the same thing. Her sister's daughter, I thought it was."

Harold shook his head. "I've seen her records down at Social Services. Neither Gracie nor her sister had any children. Both their husbands died around the same time. Gracie lived with her sister a few years, but then the sister died, too. She had no money and nowhere to go."

"Her husband owned a small business of some kind, didn't he?" Mom said. "I'm surprised she wasn't provided for after his death."

"What I heard is, he gambled most of that money away," Harold said. "Ruined his business, then started to drink. It's a sad story, but not so unusual."

Ethan and I protested. "Gracie said it wasn't her husband's fault!"

"No doubt she did say that," Harold said. "Maybe she didn't even know, or didn't want to know. When he died, Gracie had a nervous breakdown. The sister took her in and sold the house, which was all Gracie had left, to pay the debts and back taxes. Then the sister got sick, too, and there wasn't any money left. I think Gracie just tries to remember the good parts."

"Doesn't sound like there *were* too many good parts," Mom said.

"But why did she make that up about having a mean niece?" I asked Harold.

He sighed. "Sometimes people like to have one bad thing or one bad person to blame for their hardships. My guess is, Gracie doesn't want to blame her husband, and she doesn't want to think the world is so rotten it would let an old woman sleep outside in the cold, so she makes up a niece she can blame it all on."

I could understand Gracie feeling that way, but personally I was glad to find out there was no niece—I didn't like thinking that somebody who actually *knew* Gracie could be that mean to her.

Harold hoisted his big body out of the chair and headed for the kitchen. "Well, I got chicken to fry. And a frosty old heart to thaw out. And miles to go before I sleep."

Harold was such a neat person—Mr. Atchison just had to see what a great place he was running here. It occurred to me that when I'd arrived at Derby Street two weeks ago, I wasn't so sure it was a great place, either, but now that I knew a few people, I felt comfortable here. So maybe it was up to me to make Mr. Atchison feel comfortable, too. I *had* to. By the time I got finished with him, he'd think the Derby Street Shelter was more comfortable than an easy chair in front of his own fireplace. Maybe.

Chapter Eleven

Before long everything was in full swing. I was spooning soup into little bowls, and Ethan was dishing out scoops of mashed potatoes while Mom plopped chicken legs onto plates. I kept my eye out for Gracie, but I didn't see her.

Mr. Atchison had been staying in the kitchen, where Dad had tied an apron on him and put him in charge of the potato masher. I thought I actually heard him snort at a few of Harold's jokes. When things slowed down a little on the serving line, Mom went back there and got him out. "I'd like you to meet some of our regulars, Mr. Atchison," she said. He looked like she was going to make him eat turnips.

"This is Jim Greathouse," she said, making introductions as the line moved past. "Henry DuBay and Ellie MacNamara and her little guy, Petey. And, of course, Newly Puckett." Mr. Atchison nodded his head slightly at each name.

I looked up at the last name. Sure enough, there was the man who'd fished my glasses out of the muck two weeks ago. He gave me a wink, then turned to Mr.

Atchison and bowed deeply. "Mr. Atchison, sir, I'm happy to make your acquaintance. And I thank you for your help here at the shelter. The folks certainly do appreciate it." Newly Puckett smiled his big five-teeth-missing smile and took his tray off to a table. Mr. Atchison looked a little pale.

"Mr. Puckett?" I followed him to his table, in need of some help with my plan.

"Hello! It's my friend with the slippery glasses, isn't it? Call me Newly, child. Nobody calls me mister."

"Thank you. You can call me Bess."

"I'd be pleased to do that, Bess."

"Newly, do you know who that Mr. Atchison is?"

"Well, no, can't say I've ever seen him here before."

"He owns the building next door, the old Emerson Hotel, and some of the shelter people—Harold and my parents and some other people—want to buy it from him and open a place where women can sleep. since Derby Street is only for men."

"Oh, that's a wonderful idea, isn't it? You never used to see many women out there on the streets, but now, times is harder for everybody."

"The thing is, Mr. Atchison doesn't really want to sell the hotel for a shelter. He thinks it will make the downtown area worse, or bring in drugs or something. I think he's just one of those people who are scared of lots of things."

Newly nodded his head. "I see. And I suppose your mother dragged him here to try to convince him what a bunch of saints we all are."

100

"Something like that," I said.

"Saints or sinners, everybody need a place to put down his head at night."

"I know. I was thinking . . . do you know those people who sing hymns sometimes? I was hoping they might be here, but I don't know exactly who they are."

"I certainly do! And I see just what idea you comin' up with." He looked around the dining room. "There's some of them: Audrey and Juanita. And back there's John Bailey—you got to have him because he sings lower than a bass fiddle and makes all the sounds mix together so lovely. I don't see Marvin, though—he's the one usually gets people going on the singing."

"Could you do it today, Newly? Since you know them all?"

"Well, I'll surely try. Jim Greathouse is here—he's got a good voice. I'll have to be the director, though, 'cause my voice would chase laundry right off the line. You never find your long johns again." He laughed.

"Thank you, Newly."

"Don't be thankin' me, honey. You the one with the fine idea." I watched him cross from table to table, filling everybody in on who Mr. Atchison was, and how we might be able to change his mind. Pretty soon there was a group of about ten people gathered near the door, standing straight and quiet like a choir in a church. Newly posed in front of them with his hands raised.

Everybody seemed to understand that something

wonderful was about to occur. because the room got very quiet all of a sudden. When Newly brought his hands down, the choir filled the room with their voices, singing "Go Tell It on the Mountain," one of my favorite spirituals, one that we sometimes sing in church.

Considering that it was just ten people and they hadn't been practicing or anything, they sounded really good—especially with John Bailey filling in all the spaces with his low, gorgeous notes, like Newly said he would. I looked over at Mr. Atchison. It's hard to read somebody's face when you don't know him very well, but I had the feeling he was starting to get more comfortable here. Even though he wasn't actually smiling, his mouth was relaxed now, and when people started to clap along with the singing, he clapped, too.

I just felt so happy all of a sudden that, before I thought what I was doing, I ran past Newly and joined the choir. He pointed to me and smiled and nodded, then continued waving his hands around in time to the music. We told it on the mountain for about five verses, and afterward everybody clapped and whooped really loudly. The choir sang a few more quieter songs after that, and I went back to filling soup bowls. A few minutes later Mom walked by on her way to get more potatoes from the kitchen and leaned over to whisper in my ear, "You're a genius."

I was feeling pretty terrific by the time the choir all sat down again, laughing and talking to everybody on the way back to their seats. At least I was until I saw Gracie. She must have come in while we were all watching the choir. She sat alone at a table, looking really beat, and opened her garbage bag to pull out a box of Dumpster doughnuts.

"Mom, look! Gracie's here. Can I take her a tray? She looks tired."

"Sure. You can take Mr. Atchison over and introduce him, too," Mom said.

Suddenly I didn't feel like sharing Gracie with a guy who could do her a big favor without even hurting himself, and who might not do it, anyway. But he followed Mom's instructions and trudged behind me over to the table, so I didn't have much choice.

"I was surprised at first that they made you children come down here," he said.

"They don't *make* us," I said, conveniently forgetting that I'd been under orders two weeks ago and hadn't been too pleased about it. "We come because we like it here, we like doing something useful."

"Yes, well, I can see it has a certain spiritual aspect to it."

"Hi, Gracie. It's Bess," I said, putting the tray of food in front of her. I wasn't sure she'd recognize me. "This is better than doughnuts, don't you think?"

She looked up at me, and a smile spread slowly over her face. "Good girl," she said. Obviously that was my name.

"This is Mr. Atchison. Could we sit down with you a minute?"

"Sit with me," Gracie said. She picked up a chicken leg and nibbled at it without her usual gusto.

"Are you feeling okay?" I asked.

"Gracie's tired today." But she sat up straight for a minute and looked at Mr. Atchison. "Grace Jarvis Battle," she said, introducing herself the way she liked to, with all three names.

"Nice to meet you," he said, without much feeling. But then he got a funny look on his face. "You wouldn't know an Ernest Battle, would you?"

"Ernest Warren Battle. He was a good man. It wasn't his fault," she said.

"That was her husband," I said. "She talks about him a lot."

Mr. Atchison was staring at Gracie now. "Your husband was Ernest Battle? The Ernest Battle who owned Battle Textiles back in the 1960s and '70s?"

"Yessir, my Ernest. Good man. Business took him down. Wasn't his fault. Nothing left when he died."

"My goodness. Ernest and I were members of the local chamber of commerce at the same time," Mr. Atchison said. I was surprised at the way he was talking to her as if he thought she was just a regular person. "I always enjoyed his humor. I didn't realize he'd passed on."

Gracie looked up at the ceiling. "August the second, 1993. Wasn't old. Just gave up." She seemed to have forgotten all about eating.

"Don't forget your potatoes," I said.

I was glad when she started to spoon some in. Mr. Atchison asked her a few more questions, but she must have gotten tired of talking. She just shook her head and kept on eating.

He turned to me then and said in a low voice, "I met her once, years ago. She was a beautiful woman. I can still remember her smile." Mr. Atchison shook his head sadly.

That didn't make me sad, though. "I *knew* it!" I said. "I knew she was pretty. You can still tell."

Mr. Atchison wasn't too interested in what I thought. He got up and walked back into the kitchen. I kept sitting with Gracie, just to give her the company, but we didn't talk anymore, either.

She looked so small hunched over her tray. It occurred to me that she was always alone. A lot of the other guests came in groups with family or friends, but Gracie didn't seem to know anybody. She was in a world of her own. I wondered if she was lonely in that world?

Sometimes I got lonely just staying home by myself for a few hours while Willy was gone and Mom and Dad were working late. Even now, when I was beginning to understand that what they did was very important to a lot of people, I still sometimes felt kind of forgotten. Unimportant.

Was that how Gracie felt? She was *really* alone, no kids, no husband, no family. Not even her own home to be alone *in*. It made me feel sick to think about what had happened to her. Once she'd been a beautiful woman. Now she wore four layers of used clothing and slept outside. How could things like that happen?

Willy interrupted my dark thoughts. "Okay. I've scrubbed about two hundred pots, and I told Mom and Dad I'm driving you guys home now. I said we were stopping at the mall to look at CDs in case they get home before we do. So let's get this show on the road."

Gracie had finished her dinner. "Gracie, I want to show you something," I said. "A place you can stay at night. A better place than the furniture store loading dock. Will you come with us so I can show you?"

I wish I could say she looked at me with trust, like she knew I only wanted to help her. But she didn't. It was more like, *I might as well. What have I got to lose?*

I had to practically rip Ethan away from the coffee machine. He was filling large cups and chatting happily with Newly and Jim Greathouse. I waved good-bye to Mom and hoped it didn't seem strange that I was ushering Gracie ahead of me out the door.

I got into the backseat with Gracie. Wow. I had to admit, once the doors were closed, you could really smell the odor, like a bad locker room–bathroom smell. We all rolled our windows down, but nobody said anything. After all, she couldn't help it. They don't have showers out back of Montoni's Furniture store.

Willy raced up to the middle school, fanning himself as he drove. We directed him around to the back parking lot, which was deserted on a Sunday afternoon; he pulled up close to The Zone Annex. Ethan and I got out quickly and helped Gracie. He carried her garbage bag, and I got two old blankets that I'd sneaked from our attic out of the trunk.

Sure enough, the lock on the shed was broken. Ethan showed Gracie several times how to slip it open, and explained to her that when she left The Annex, she'd have to put it back so it looked like it was locked. She seemed to be listening to him carefully, but it was hard to tell if she really understood everything.

Inside The Annex there were only some unused flats and a few broken-down chairs. The floor was made of wood, but I hoped the blankets would warm it up a little bit. I also hoped no rats or other creatures could get in; the thought of it made me feel queasy.

We tried to explain to Gracie that she could stay in the shed at night or on the weekends, but she would have to leave when the sun came up during the week, so no students or teachers caught her there. We told her we'd bring food when we could.

She kept nodding, so we decided she must have understood pretty much all of what we'd said. Once, when we were showing her how she ought to leave the blankets hidden behind the flats in the mornings, she looked right at Ethan and said, "Jesus wants me for his rainbow, yes sirree!"

Ethan was worried because he thought she hadn't been listening to him, but then she kind of knocked on the wall and said, "Good little house. Gracie has a good little house now."

There wasn't much else to do except hope that nobody found her there. I wished I'd thought of bringing her a pillow. Maybe I could get Willy to drive me back some evening. If I could come up with another bribe.

Ethan told her one more time that she'd have to leave when the sun came up, and she nodded. "Gracie knows. She walks around in the daytime."

She stayed when we left, so we figured she'd understood that much at least. She even waved to us from the doorway, like it really was a good little house we'd given her. But I didn't feel good about it. I felt exhausted and depressed. What *had* we given her, really? A falling-down shack and two thin blankets. She'd have to spend all day tomorrow, and the next day and the next, walking around, trying to keep warm and dry, waiting until it was dark enough to go back to her shack. The more I got to know Gracie, the more I understood how terrible her life really was. And there was so little I could do to help.

Willy had all the car doors open when we got back, airing out his heap. "I'll have to spray with deodorizer before I let Caroline get in here," he complained. "So, Mother Teresa, can we get on with our lives now?"

"Shut up, Willy! I hate you!" I hadn't meant to say that—it just came out. I guess Willy was surprised, too. For the first time in his life, he didn't say anything back to me. As a matter of fact, none of us said a word the whole ride home.

Chapter Twelve

Both Ethan and I were tired and grouchy Monday afternoon as we waited for Mom to pick us up after rehearsal. It had been a long afternoon. Ms. Plumbly had insisted on rehearsing the park scene over and over, and since the tree scenery wasn't ready to be put onstage yet, I was a stand-in for the biggest tree so the kids could get used to where it would be. Everybody thought that was hysterical. They pretended to climb me, carve their initials in me, pick my leaves off. I was just lucky there was no dog in the cast.

Ethan had had a rough afternoon, too. Apparently he'd sneaked away from the flat painters to take a look in the one window of The Zone Annex. He saw Gracie's blankets and other stuff shoved into a corner, so he figured she'd gotten the idea about coming and going, anyway, if not about hiding her things.

But just then he heard Jake yelling, "Hey, you! What are you doing?"

"Nothing," Ethan said. "Just taking a break, walking around." He tried to pretend he wasn't nervous as a dog in a thunderstorm.

"Oh, it's you," Jake said. "Okay. Somebody's been messing with that lock. I just wanted to make sure you weren't some kid sneaking in to smoke cigarettes. With all that old canvas in there, the place could easily burn down."

I felt kind of sick when Ethan told me. "It could? We put her in a place that could burn down?"

"She doesn't smoke, does she? She couldn't afford to buy cigarettes, could she?" Ethan was sitting on the steps with his head resting on his knees like it was too heavy to hold up anymore. He groaned.

"She won't burn it down," I said after I thought it over for a minute. "If no middle school kid has burned it by now, Gracie won't. But I think we should stay away from The Annex. What if Jake checks inside and finds her stuff? Even if he just goes inside, he'll, you know, *smell* her. He'll know something's going on, even if he doesn't know what, and he'll figure out we're involved."

"Yeah," Ethan agreed. "We don't want Gracie to lose her little house."

I started to imagine what would happen if Jake put the whole thing together. I knew he wasn't exactly crazy about me now, but at least he acknowledged me, at least he thought I was relatively competent at my job as stage manager. What if he knew I was part of a scheme to hide a homeless person on school property? I mean, she looks so crazy—people wouldn't understand at first. They'd think . . . there was something wrong with *me*.

"What would our friends think." I said to Ethan, "if they found out we were hiding an old lady out there?"

"Gracie, not just some old lady."

"I know, but they'd think we were pretty nuts!"

"Who would?"

"Our friends! The kids from the play!" I said.

Ethan gave me a funny look. "First of all, I don't really think of most of those kids as friends—I hardly know them. And second of all, how come you care so much what everybody thinks?"

Why did Ethan always have to be so *right* about everything? Maybe it was shallow of me, but I didn't want Jake, or anybody, to think I hung around with smelly old women. Of course, I knew Gracie was more than that, but *they* didn't know it.

"What if we got in trouble for it, and they made us quit the play?" I asked him. I knew he enjoyed working backstage now.

But as usual, he just shrugged. "Then we'd quit the play. Gracie's more important than a play, isn't she?"

I felt bad that I couldn't immediately say, *Yes, of course, you're right, Ethan*. But I couldn't. It seemed like time to worry about myself a little bit now.

Mom drove up just then, so I didn't have to answer him, anyway. She had her head sticking out the window and she was yelling as she pulled up. "We got it! We bought the Emerson Hotel! Signed the papers this afternoon!"

Ethan and I started yelling, too, as we climbed into the backseat. "How? Really? Did Atchison give in? Why?" We asked her a million questions.

"We're not sure, to tell you the truth. I think maybe it was the choir singing, or the camaraderie back in the kitchen, but Harold swears it was meeting Gracie that really convinced him. Either way, you get a lot of the credit, Bess."

That would have made me feel good, if I hadn't just been the one who wasn't sure Gracie was more important than a middle school *play*. I gave Ethan a guilty smile as he patted me on the back. "How soon can the new shelter be opened?" Ethan asked.

"Well, there's some repair work to do, and we have to use volunteer labor as much as possible to keep our costs down. But we're aiming for Thanksgiving weekend, which is only five weeks away. I think we can manage it if we work like crazy. It worries me that it's getting cold so early this year. I hate to think of the women outside on these windy nights."

Ethan and I exchanged secret looks. At least we'd managed to do that much. At least Gracie was inside, out of the wind.

"There are already beds in the rooms, left over from the hotel," Mom continued. "Most of them are fine, though some of the mattresses have to be replaced. The sponsors will all help, of course, but we'll still need to raise more money to keep things running. We'll also need donations of sheets and blankets and towels, that kind of thing."

"We could collect things at school," Ethan said excitedly. "It could be like a club. What do you think?" He beamed at me.

"Maybe," I said, imagining the two of us sitting behind a table with a sign saying, DORKS DOING GOOD DEEDS. I mean, it was one thing to help out at the shelter, but did we have to announce it at school? One look at Ethan's face told me our secret was about to go public whether I liked it or not.

"Maybe you could!" Mom said. "Good idea, Ethan. You'd need to get a teacher to sponsor you, and you'd need someplace to store donations until I could pick them up. We can keep stuff in our dining room until the shelter opens. . . ." Mom was off and running, as usual.

So what if we wouldn't be able to use our dining room for another month? We'd all be too busy to sit down to a meal together, anyway! Really, did we have to spend every single minute helping other people? And how come it's always *my* family who are the weirdos leading every crusade? I mean, Ethan thought this was so great, but he could sit and collect blankets at school, and then go home to beef stew and homemade biscuits, served at an actual table, by a mother who couldn't wait to hear what her children had been doing all day.

Listening to Mom and Ethan tossing ideas back and forth made me think we should have been born into each other's families. They just assumed I'd be perfectly happy to be part of it all, and I realized if I wanted to see either of them in the next five weeks, I'd have to be. And, of course, I *did* want to help Gracie—now that I knew her, I could never forget about her again. But still, raising money for a homeless shelter was not like starting a literary magazine or getting kids to crew for the play, or even raising money for a sporting event. There was just nothing cool about it.

By the beginning of the next week, we had permission from the principal and had signed up Mr. Kline, the sixth-grade social studies teacher, as our sponsor. We had the use of several shelves in the custodian's closet in the cafeteria as long as Mom promised to pick up donations every Friday afternoon. The campaign was set to start that Friday during lunch, so Ethan and I planned to make signs after school on Tuesday, and then have Mr. Kline announce it on the public address system Wednesday morning. We were calling the organization the Women's Shelter Aid Society.

I had managed to get a little more excited about it during the week, since I didn't have much choice. I thought maybe we could get a few other kids interested, too, so I started with the obvious one. "Can you help us this afternoon?" I asked Janette. "We're working at my house. Mom bought poster board and markers."

"I can't," she said. "Violin."

"I thought your lesson wasn't until five," Ethan pointed out. We knew Janette's busy schedule as well as she did. "You could help before that."

Janette sighed. "Why can't we just do the things we used to? I mean, just hang out together and play board games or something?"

What was she talking about? "You don't like to play games."

"Well, then, you could play and I'd watch. I don't feel like *doing* anything when I have a few hours free. My whole life is filled up with *doing* things."

"But this is *important,*" I said, as if there was nothing I'd rather be doing myself. "It's not like violin lessons or jazz dancing or one of those dumb things. Besides, board games are childish. They're for kids."

"First of all, violin isn't *dumb.* And what's wrong with being childish? I feel like I never even got to be a kid!" Janette actually sounded angry, which I'm sure I've never heard her be before. "I wish my mother had had another child so the two of us could have been kids together! I'm tired of being a little adult."

After her outburst, she blushed. Actually I thought it was pretty cool that she was finally speaking up for herself.

"Okay," I said. "So on Saturday afternoon we'll get together and do something really *childish.*"

Janette sighed. "I can't Saturday. I sort of have plans of my own that day." She looked slightly guilty.

I was amazed. Janette never did anything except with

115

her mother or us. Had she made a new friend? "Well, what are you doing?"

She giggled a little and blushed again. "You won't believe this, but you know Jake, the set director? He's coming over on Saturday, and we're going to take a walk downtown or something, maybe get a pizza."

I stopped walking, stunned. "What? You're going on a date with Jake?"

"It's not exactly a date. I mean, it's in the afternoon."

I felt like I'd just thrown up my dinner—weak and empty, but still sick. "If you're going out for pizza, it's a *date*, Janette—don't be stupid."

I could see she was surprised I'd say something so mean to her, and so was Ethan. "What's with you?" he asked me.

Of course I knew I didn't have any right to be mad at Janette. It's not as if Jake had ever really noticed me; about the only thing he'd ever said to me was, "Get your scarf out of my face." But still, I *liked* him, and it's hard when somebody you like prefers one of your best friends. It's hard not to be mad at *her*.

"Well, Janette," I said, trying to calm down a little bit, "I mean, you're only in the sixth grade! Dating is not exactly a *childish* activity, is it? I can't believe your mother is letting you go out with an eighth grader!"

"Are you kidding?" Janette said with a sarcastic laugh. "My mother is thrilled. I guess she thinks I'll be a prodigy at dating if I can't do anything else."

Ethan looked worried. "But you do *want* to go out with him, don't you? I mean, you aren't just doing it because your mother wants you to? Like with ballet lessons?"

I was pretty sure Ethan was still in the dark about the whole *reason* for dating, but at least he was being a friend to Janette, which was more than I could manage at the moment.

"No, I wouldn't go out with him just for my mother's sake. He's really nice, don't you think?"

"Yeah, I like him okay," Ethan said. "Don't you, Bess?"

I shrugged. "I don't know him very well."

"The thing is," Janette continued, "I get so nervous. I mean, it's one thing to talk to him about painting flats, but what can I talk about for a whole afternoon?"

Ethan was thoughtful. "You could ask him about other plays he's worked on. What teachers are good in seventh and eighth grade. If he has any brothers or sisters. That kind of stuff."

"That's good! Thanks, Ethan," Janette said. "If only I can remember it when I'm nervous."

Before long Janette left, and Ethan and I went to get our bikes. I love riding bikes with Ethan—we don't talk much, just fly along the street together, thinking our own thoughts.

One thing I was thinking was: I wouldn't know how to talk to Jake, either, but I sure wish it were my problem instead of Janette's. And another was: How weird is it to be talking about dating with Janette and Ethan? For all the years I'd known them, this topic had never come up. But now it was probably going to, more and more. What if we became just like Willy and his friends, so idiotic about the opposite sex? But then, Ethan *was* the opposite sex—did that mean someday he wouldn't want to be my best friend?

I didn't see why growing up had to be such a big deal. Why couldn't things just go along smoothly like they had so far? Janette going out with Jake was bad enough, but what if Ethan showed up with a girlfriend one of these days? I mean, he probably wasn't ready for that yet, but how long before he was? Already he'd changed from sweatshirts and sweatpants to T-shirts and jeans. And what would happen to me when some girl started hanging on to Ethan's arm and giggling? Would she let me hang out with them? Would he? Would they want to play Monopoly or ride bikes? Fat chance.

I sighed, and Ethan looked in my direction, then pulled his bike over closer. "You like Jake, too, don't you?" he asked. Maybe he'd been thinking about the same things I was.

"No!" I said. "He's too old. Besides, he probably doesn't even like to ride bikes."

Chapter Thirteen

I'm not going down there again," Willy said. "And you're going to be in big trouble when people find out about this."

"Nobody's going to find out about it. Please, Willy, just this once!" I begged.

"Get a hearing aid, kiddo." He walked out to his car, and I followed him. The thing was, I couldn't figure out how to get food to Gracie during the week. I wasn't going to carry stuff to school with me—I'd look like an idiot lugging bags of apples and loaves of bread around all day—and even if I did, I was afraid somebody would see me going into The Annex in the daytime.

Ethan and I were getting busier and busier with the play. Ms. Plumbly said Ethan could be assistant stage manager, and we were supposed to be at rehearsals most of the day Saturday. We didn't have time to ride to the supermarket first, and Gracie wouldn't be there that early, anyway. We were getting worried. What if she didn't have enough to eat? What if she thought we'd forgotten about her?

Sometimes I almost wished I'd never gone to the shelter in the first place, never even met Gracie. I mean, once you know how bad things are for somebody, it's hard to forget it. Here I had all this work to do for the play, and instead I was worrying about Gracie and feeling guilty. I wished there were other people who were worried, too—Ms. Plumbly or Jake or Kimberly Pringle. If more people were worried, I wouldn't have to do so much worrying myself.

The only way I could think of to get food to Gracie was to have Willy drive me down there at night. I could say he was taking me to the library. We'd stop at the supermarket and then take the food over to her at The Annex. It would be simple, if Willy were a human being.

Bribery had worked once, maybe it would again. And if not bribery, maybe sabotage. I followed Willy outside.

"How's it going with Caroline?" I asked loudly.

Willy was just opening the car door. He whirled around and gaped at me. "Shut up!" he whispered. "She'll hear you!" He glanced quickly at the house next door.

"I was just wondering. I mean, Ethan and I went to a lot of trouble to get you a date—"

"And then I did you a favor. The deal's over."

"I know, but I need to take Gracie some food. You probably wouldn't want Caroline to know you wouldn't even help me feed a poor, hungry old lady who has to live in a shed—"

"I don't care what you say to Caroline, okay? I only went out with her once. She isn't interested in me. Are you happy now?"

Willy got in his car and slammed the door, then hung his arms over the steering wheel and stared out the front window, looking like his hamster had just died. Who would have believed a girl could turn my bully of a brother into this miserable mess? He was a sad sight.

"Did you ask her to go out with you again?" I was almost afraid to ask.

"No," he said grumpily.

"Then how do you know she wouldn't?"

"I just know, okay? I'm a mind reader."

"Do you want me and Ethan to talk to her again?"

"No! Absolutely not! She'll really think I'm an idiot!" Willy pounded his head on the steering wheel.

"I think you ought to ask her out again. She said you were cute."

He stopped pounding. "She did?"

"I told you that."

"I couldn't think of anything to say to her. There's nothing interesting about me."

"That's true, but you could talk about your fabulous younger sister," I suggested.

He gave me a disgusted look.

"You could talk about the shelter. That's interesting. She's probably never been there."

"I'd bet on that."

"It would at least make you *seem* like a kind person," I said.

"Thanks."

"Janette's going on a date," I said, feeling like a brave little toaster just for bringing it up. "She couldn't think of anything to say to . . . her date, and Ethan told her to talk about stuff like what teachers were good. You could tell Caroline who she should take next year or something."

Willy snorted, then laughed. "*Hey, Caroline, if you go out with me again, I'll give you the lowdown on the high school physics faculty!* Yeah, that would knock her socks off." He shook his head. "You're too much. Okay. Run in and give Mom some excuse. But this better not take too long."

Yes! After handing Mom the library story, which she barely listened to (no surprise—she was on the phone), I ran upstairs to get some money. I was afraid Mom would notice if I kept taking it from the Emergency Jar, so I took ten dollars from the money I'd earned last summer walking the Hofmeisters' dog while they were on vacation. They'd given me thirty-five dollars, and I'd been saving it for something special—I guess Gracie was it. I grabbed a pillow off the front porch as I came back out; nobody would ever miss it.

We stopped at the supermarket, and I got juice and bread and peanut butter and a small bag of apples. Ten dollars doesn't go too far in a grocery store.

Willy parked the car in the lot near The Annex, and I got out. Then, so did he.

"You can wait in the car if you want," I said.

He shrugged and took the pillow from me. "It's dark. I'll go with you."

I was kind of glad Willy came, too. The door to The Annex was in the shadow of the parking lot lights, and it was a little creepy to open it up and walk inside in the dark.

"Gracie! It's me, Bess." I didn't want to scare her. "Good girl."

I heard something moving, but I couldn't see a thing in the dark. What if there were rats in here? My legs got kind of shaky when I imagined what sorts of things might be getting ready to dash across my feet. "Are you in here?" I called again.

"Phew! Something's in here," Willy said. The shed did smell bad, like the Dumpster at the supermarket only all locked up in a tiny space.

"Good girl got food?" The little voice came from the corner. I was so relieved, I dropped the bag of apples, and they went rolling around the floor.

"Oh, those are the apples." My eyes were beginning to be able to see shapes in the dark. One apple rolled up to Gracie's thin body where she sat on the blankets in the corner. She picked it up and began to chomp away.

"We brought other stuff, too," I said, showing her the food. "And a pillow." Willy stepped forward and handed her the pillow.

"Good boy," Gracie said, smiling up at Willy. I didn't try to explain that this was a different good boy than last time.

"Are you doing all right in here? Is it comfortable

enough?" I asked, thinking how moronic it was to ask an old woman if she was comfortable sleeping on a floor in an unheated shed.

"There's going to be a women's shelter pretty soon. Then you'll be inside at night. You won't have to sleep in this shed. You'll be warm." How could I make her understand?

She sat up a little straighter. "Grace Jarvis Battle," she said. She liked her name a lot.

"She's out of it," Willy said. "She doesn't know what you're saying. Let's go."

But then Gracie started talking again. "Grace Jarvis Battle lived in a big house. She had a red-and-black rug in the parlor with peacocks woven into each corner." She put her arms together from the elbows to the wrists and then spread them open at the top, like a peacock's tail. I could almost see that rug myself.

"On cold nights, Ernest made a fire in the fireplace," she continued. "When my father came for dinner, I cooked a leg of lamb. Yes sirree, the reverend loved his leg of lamb. And I loved the reverend." Then she went back to eating her apple.

Willy and I stood there a few more minutes, waiting to hear more, but that was all there was. I told her I'd try to bring her more food in a few days, but I guess she was too interested in this stuff to plan ahead.

She waved to us as we went out, and I pulled the heavy door shut behind us. We walked back to the car in silence and got in, but Willy didn't start it up right away. Finally he said, "How can she stand to smell like that?"

"What choice does she have?" I said, feeling suddenly angry at him. "She can't exactly take a bath, can she?"

"I know. I just meant, jeez, how does she even go to the bathroom?"

"I don't know," I said, not wanting to think about it.

"You see bums like that in the library sometimes. They fall asleep in the chairs." He didn't say it meanly, but it made me cry, anyway. Me, who never cries.

"She's not a bum, Willy! She had rotten luck! She had a red peacock rug in her parlor! She was like our grandmothers! What if this happened to them?"

"I know. I know." Willy rolled down his window and leaned way out like he was studying the sky so I could wipe up my face without an audience.

Chapter Fourteen

The next few weeks were so busy, it seemed like I was always supposed to be in two places at the same time. Mom said I was passing myself coming and going, but then, she was, too, working at her job and trying to get the new shelter ready to open. Now that I was so busy myself, it didn't bother me so much that Mom and Dad were busy, too; I didn't have time for them, either. Besides, the more we all worked, the sooner the shelter would be finished. True, dinner was mostly soup from a can or scrambled eggs or tuna fish sandwiches, and we were lucky to have three out of four family members present, but there wasn't a dining-room table to eat on, anyway, since it was buried under piles of blankets and towels for the shelter.

Bye Bye Birdie was finally "on its feet," and we had rehearsals every day after school. Ms. Plumbly gave me a lot of responsibility, like she'd said she would. She sat in the front row of the theater, or paced up and down the aisle, while I was in charge of everything backstage, curtain and lighting people, set changes, props, and all those giggling, blabbering actors who seemed to think nobody else was as important as they were.

It turned out that the lead girl, Dara Washburne, who played Kim, and the lead boy, Mitchell Montana, who played Conrad Birdie, hated each other. Mitchell had once dated Dara's best friend and hurt her feelings when they broke up, so Dara refused to speak to him. Of course, in the play she was supposed to be madly in love with him, so this was a little problem.

Ms. Plumbly kept saying, "Dara, you *adore* him! You swoon when he *looks* at you!"

Dara kept rolling her eyes and saying, "I'm glad I wasn't born in the fifties. Girls were so *dumb* then." I had to admit she was right. I couldn't imagine throwing myself at some guy's feet, screaming and fainting.

"Pretend he's Billy Joel or somebody!" Ms. Plumbly said.

"Billy Joel?" Dara said. "My *mother* listens to Billy Joel!"

"Well, who do you listen to?" Ms. Plumbly tried again.

Dara shrugged. "Black Pillow, Dime-store Chickens, The Jam Heads."

Ms. Plumbly stared at her blankly. "Dime-store Chickens. Well, just try to remember you're acting, okay? Let's run through it again."

We had to go over and over the scene where Conrad gives Kim his "one last kiss," and then her boyfriend, Hugo, played by Jeremy Spooner, a skinny sixth grader, hits Conrad in the face and knocks him down. Dara kept screwing her face up like *she'd* just been hit every time Conrad Birdie kissed her, and Hugo didn't really seem to care one way or the other, which made his punch seem more like an accident than anger.

Meanwhile, Kimberly Pringle and the other girls playing teenyboppers in love kept screaming, and singing, "We love you, Conrad," in high, screechy voices, until everybody who wasn't singing started complaining they had a headache.

Now that the sets were all built, Jake didn't have to hang around at all the rehearsals, but he did, anyway. He *said* it was in case there were any problems with those old flats standing up. But I'd been there when he'd reinforced them with plywood, and he'd told me how to fix it if one of them started to buckle, which was about the longest conversation I'd ever had with him.

No, I had a feeling his presence had more to do with the fact that Janette had decided to play her violin in the orchestra, because now that they were practicing every day, too, Jake was spending an awful lot of time in the front-row seat closest to the violin section, staring.

"So," I said to Janette, "you're not nervous about being in the orchestra?"

She smiled. "Well, you know, we sit down there in a dark hole under the stage. People can hardly even see us."

"I'm surprised your mom is letting you skip all your tennis and ballet lessons."

"She's happy I'm showing off my violin talent. She's

invited everyone on planet Earth to come and see me, which is funny, since I'm invisible." She laughed.

The really funny thing was, Janette *wasn't* invisible anymore. She'd been very different the last few weeks, still a little jumpy, of course, but not so ready to disappear down a rabbit hole the minute somebody looked at her. When Jake walked up behind her and put his hands on her shoulders, she gave a happy little shriek, and I didn't know where to look. For sure not at this googly-eyed twosome.

"Did I scare you?" he said.

"Yes!" she said, laughing and tilting her head toward his shoulder.

"Sorry." He put his arm around her shoulder and quickly gave her a little hug. She shivered nervously, but I could tell she was enjoying it immensely. I would have, too.

"See you later," I said, although she was paying about as much attention to me as my mother does when she's in the middle of one of her projects. I slunk off backstage to look for Ethan.

If only it didn't make me feel so bad to see Jake and Janette together, but it did, and there wasn't much I could do about it. When he looked at her like he wanted to lick her face, it made my stomach flop over. I guess I'd never liked a boy that way before, and it made me feel like a dumb little kid when he didn't even notice me standing right there next to Janette. I didn't like the way this system worked—that you could be crazy about somebody at the same time that he was crazy about somebody else. Who came up with *that* idea?

Ethan wasn't too comfortable with Janette's change, either. He insisted we ride our bikes to school even on cold days so we wouldn't have to ride home with her after school. It was like she was a different person now, and we didn't know what to say to her.

Even Kimberly Pringle commented on it. "Little Janette sure grew up fast, didn't she?"

I was busy guiding one set of flats offstage and another set on, but I took the time to give her a look. "What's that supposed to mean?"

She shrugged. "Just that she's kind of outgrown you and your teddy bear, Ethan." I walked away, but she followed me. "You know, Bess, you could be cool if you'd ditch him. He is so dweeby. I mean, this year you're doing stuff, like this play, and with your new clothes and everything—even though they aren't what *I'd* wear—you've become kind of a . . . real person."

"What was I before?" I asked, pushing her out of the way of a moving tree. "Part of the scenery?"

She grinned. "You know what I mean. You could be almost popular if you started hanging around with the right kids instead of collecting hand-me-downs with Chubby every lunch period."

My first instinct was to belt her; that was *usually* my first instinct when I spoke to Kimberly. The thing was, it sounded like she was offering me something, a chance to hang around with her friends, the popular kids, and I wasn't sure I wanted to blow it off too quickly. Not that I'd *ever* give up my friendship with Ethan, but maybe, if I got in good with the popular kids, I could bring Ethan in later on, too.

"Who exactly are the right kids, Kimberly?"

"As if you don't know," she said. "*My* group: Kitty and Elizabeth and Russell and Chris and Peter . . ."

I didn't even know those kids. But I did know that Kitty English was gorgeous, and Russell Turner was a god of some sort, and Elizabeth Parker never spoke to *anyone,* and Kimberly Pringle drove me crazy.

"So, if you want to go to the movies with us on Friday night, you can. I'll call you," Kimberly was saying.

She was actually *inviting* me. Now what? I imagined myself standing in line at the Warburton Theater trying to think of something witty to say to Kitty English, being ignored by Elizabeth Parker, and probably all the rest of them, too, unless I could figure out how to act cool in the next three days. Of course, other kids might see me with these kids, and then . . . and then what? Then I'd have to spend another night going to the movies with a bunch of other kids I didn't really like? The whole idea suddenly seemed ridiculous. I didn't *want* to hang out with those kids.

"The thing is, I'm awfully busy lately, with the play and the women's shelter and everything."

Kimberly stuck out her hip and planted her fist on it. "You're going to have to drop that women's shelter thing. It's so creepy: collecting moth-eaten blankets for a bunch of old bag ladies whose own children don't even want them."

I stared at her. I could have guessed that's what Kimberly and her friends would think about the shelter, but now that I'd actually heard the words come out of her mouth, I couldn't imagine why I'd ever cared what people like her thought. Why would I even consider spending time with this person? I smiled. "Kimberly, I'd much rather drop you."

"What?"

"Well, Chubby and I really prefer old bag ladies to young snobs."

Her face froze up like Alaska. "Your loss," she said, and stalked off.

I watched Kimberly's hair swing from side to side as she marched away from me. I'd probably just blown my one chance to be somebody people noticed. Maybe I could have gotten used to Kimberly. Maybe those other kids weren't really so bad. Maybe they'd eventually like Ethan. Although it didn't seem very likely. Nope. Kimberly had explained my choice clearly: If I wanted to be cool, I had to give up my uncool friends. Crud. If being popular meant having to hang around with people like Kimberly, I'd rather be the queen of the dweebs. But why couldn't Ethan and I be *popular* dweebs?

Some days the rehearsals were a total disaster. It seemed like we'd never get everybody doing the right thing at the right time. Girls who'd done a dance perfectly for weeks suddenly started bumping into each other and collapsing in a giggling heap. Except for the girl who broke her toe dancing into a table leg; she wasn't laughing. The box of telephones got lost again, and Amy finally located it under a pile of poodle skirts that had been dumped in the boys' dressing room by mistake. A bunch of kids got the flu; Jeremy Spooner threw up. Dara Washburne burst into tears when someone accused her of liking Mitchell Montana, who had suddenly come down with laryngitis.

Sometimes, if I'd been at the shelter over the weekend, I'd kind of forget where I was for a minute. The middle school actors would morph into the soup kitchen guests. The noise level was about the same. Jeremy Spooner looked a lot like Newly Puckett if you squinted your eyes. And maybe if Mitchell Montana had to fight in a terrible war, he'd come back sad and kind of broken up like Jim Greathouse. And what if Kimberly Pringle got pregnant in high school and her boyfriend left and her parents threw her out? She'd be like Ellie MacNamara, who slept in her car with her little boy, Petey. Sometimes it seemed like only luck and a few years separated us from them.

"Well," Ms. Plumbly said one afternoon after a terrible rehearsal, "it's always darkest before the dawn. The last week or so always seems impossible, but it gets pulled together at the last minute." She gave an optimistic smile.

"Always?" I asked.

Her smile twitched. "Well, almost always. Don't worry, Bess. We'll pull it off."

I hated to make more problems for her, but I had something to tell her. "Ms. Plumbly? About next Saturday?"

"Rehearsals all day! We'll whip it into shape. Then dress rehearsals Wednesday and Thursday of next week. Friday and Saturday we're on! It's exciting, isn't it?"

I nodded. "The only thing is, I can't be here Saturday morning."

"But Bess, you're our stage manager. You've got to be here! You've made a commitment!"

"I know, Ms. Plumbly, but I made another commitment, too. You know about the Women's Shelter Aid Society? I collect money and blankets and things at lunch period."

"Yes, I've seen you at that table. I confess I haven't taken the time to find out what it's all about."

"My mother and some other people who work at the Derby Street Shelter are opening a new shelter, one for women. It opens Thanksgiving Day, and Ethan and I are helping out."

"Well, Bess, that sounds like a wonderful project. But it doesn't sound like something that has to be done on Saturday. Now the play—"

"But it *does*. Saturday is painting day at the new shelter. We need lots of people to get the whole shelter painted in one day. It starts at eight o'clock in the morning and goes all day, but I'll leave at one o'clock and come here. My mom will drive me over."

"Bess, when you signed on to be stage manager, you made a commitment to me and to the other cast members. This play is very important to them." She looked stern.

"I know it is," I told her, "but the shelter is even more important to more people."

"Well, I see you've made your choice," Ms. Plumbly said stiffly, turning her back to me. Didn't she understand what I was saying?

I tried once more. "Ms. Plumbly, if we don't get the shelter ready, people will have to sleep outside in the winter. The play's not *that* kind of important."

She sighed. "Bess, I fail to see how your painting a wall or not will make all that much difference. I know you want to be a part of what's going on at the shelter, but I still think the play should be your first priority right now."

"As long as you're mad anyway, I might as well tell you that Ethan's coming to the shelter on Saturday morning, too."

She just shook her head. "Hit 'em while they're down," was all she said.

"I already asked Amy to cover for me. She's backstage all the time, anyway. She can do it for a few hours."

"It's not Amy's job." Ms. Plumbly had never been mad at me before, and I didn't like it at all. Her voice got very quiet and small, like she didn't even want to give me any words.

I thought if I could get her to laugh, she wouldn't be so mad, so I said, "I don't suppose you'd like to make a donation to the Women's Shelter Aid Society, would you?" Ms. Plumbly was usually so easy to get along with that almost any attempt at humor would break her up.

But this time she didn't even look up from the book she'd opened. "Not at the moment, no. I think you should go now, Bess," she said.

So I did. It's funny how you can feel guilty even when you think you did the right thing.

Chapter Fifteen

I'd managed to talk Willy into driving me down to The Zone Annex on Thursday nights so I could take Gracie a little food. Mom and Dad had so many night meetings themselves, I didn't have to lie very often. Willy wasn't crazy about it, of course, but it was getting to be kind of a habit. He didn't like to go into The Annex, though—he couldn't stand the smell. So he'd park the car where the headlights lit up the shed a little bit. Then he'd just sit in the car and wait for me.

It was funny. He acted like he hated doing it, but I'm not sure that was true. One night I had a big science project due, and Gracie sort of slipped my mind. At nine o'clock Willy knocked on my door. "Hey, aren't you gonna go feed the old lady?" he muttered.

I stared at him. "Willy, I forgot! And now it's so late already!"

"Hurry up. We'll do a fast one. I'm busy, too, you know."

But if he was so busy, he didn't have to mention it. I didn't even feel like going myself. My B in science was quickly heading for a C, so this project *had* to be good.

But we went, both of us mumbling that night about having other things to do. The fact that it was raining and I got soaked running in and out of the supermarket and then The Annex didn't help my mood any, either. At least Gracie wasn't getting wet, I kept reminding myself.

Willy wouldn't go to the Derby Street Shelter on Sundays, though. He said he'd done it twice and that was plenty. He said he wasn't a welfare worker.

Ethan and I went regularly now, every two weeks with Mom and Dad. Ethan's mom went whenever she could, too. You could tell she was the type who'd enjoy it. She learned everybody's name right away, and people would come up and compliment her on the food, even though she worked on the line and didn't actually cook any of it. As a matter of fact, she *refused* to cook. "I do too much of that at home," she said. "Here I just like to be out with the people."

A lot of the Derby Street volunteers were coming to painting day. And Mom had talked some kids from the high school into coming down to work for a few hours, too. Harold said a lot of the Derby Street "regulars" would be there, like Jim Greathouse and Newly Puckett. I tried to talk Janette into coming, too, but she looked at me like I'd suggested eating cat food.

"You know my mother would never let me go to that area of town," she said.

"Why not? *My* mother will be there. It's daytime. What does she think will happen to you?"

"I don't know. I don't think she'd like me hanging around with those people."

She was studying the sole of one shoe as if there were a cryptic message written on it, or maybe dog doo or something. It occurred to me that Janette had no idea what her mother would say about going to the shelter, and she had no intention of finding out.

"You just don't want to go, do you? You're blaming your mother, but it's you who's scared."

Janette looked up at me, annoyed. "I'm not like you, Bess. I'm not good in new situations, with new people. Especially someplace like that."

"Someplace like what?"

"Like a shelter where there are all kinds of weirdos!"

I thought of Gracie sitting at the table, telling everybody her whole long name, Grace Jarvis Battle, and saying how it wasn't her husband's fault. How could Janette call people names when she didn't even know them!

"Guess what, Janette? Those *weirdos* are just people! Some of them are poor, and some of them had bad luck, but that doesn't make them skunks or rats! They're still human beings!"

"Why do you have to make me feel bad about it? I'm sorry, but I just can't do it!" She turned and walked off, just like that.

I tried not to think about the man whose teeth fell into the garbage, and how I'd freaked out about it and wouldn't go back to the shelter for years. But that was when I was a little kid and didn't understand things. If only I could introduce Janette to Gracie, she'd see how it really was.

Ethan's mom was disappointed she couldn't make it on Saturday. Her husband was going on a business trip, and she couldn't very well bring a two-year-old and a five-year-old along if she planned to get any painting done.

"She asked Amanda and Caroline if they'd baby-sit, but Amanda's going to a soccer banquet that day," Ethan told me. "And guess what Caroline said? *She* wants to come to painting day! She even asked me if there was room for her to go in your car."

"She did? That's strange. I thought she was mostly interested in playing with her hair and meeting boys."

"Me too. I said I'd ask you, though."

"Wait a minute!" I stopped my bike in the middle of the street as the truth began to trickle down into my brain cells. "I know why she wants to come. It's Willy! She thinks Willy will be there!"

Ethan thought about it. "Could be. I heard her telling my mom that Willy was quiet, but sweet."

"*Sweet?* Not in my lifetime."

"I think they were trying to figure out why Willy never called her again after that one time they went out. Mom said maybe her looks scared him off. She meant because Caroline's so good-looking, but I said, 'Boy, they certainly would scare *me* off." Then they shooed me away, and I didn't hear any more."

"Can I tell him?"

"I don't care."

So I waited until later that night as Willy and I were driving to the supermarket for apples and bread, our usual Thursday destination.

"Guess who's coming to help paint the women's shelter on Saturday?"

"Jerry Seinfeld? Nelson Mandela? The Artist Formerly Known as Prince?"

He thought he was so hysterical.

"Caroline Riley," I said. "She wants to ride with us."

"What?" The car skidded to one side a little. "Why would Caroline Riley want to waste her day painting some old hotel?"

"That's what I said, too, but then I figured it out."

"Figured what out?"

"She thinks *you'll* be there."

There was a long silence. I was beginning to think he hadn't understood me, when he muttered, "Sure. That's likely." He pulled into the supermarket parking lot and slumped over the steering wheel like his muscles had turned to pudding. All you had to do was mention this girl's name and he melted into a puddle. Her power was awe-inspiring.

I figured I'd better give him the good news before he disintegrated completely. "Ethan heard her telling her mother she wished you'd called her back after your date. And here's your Christmas present: She thinks you're *sweet*."

Willy stared at me with little, round rodent eyes. I'd never seen a look like that on his face before. I couldn't tell if it was pain or fear or nausea. "Are you okay? You aren't going to get sick, are you?" I asked.

He turned away. "Did she really say that?"

"Ethan wouldn't lie about it. He doesn't care enough to lie."

"What should I do?"

What should he do? My know-it-all big brother was asking *me* what he should do? It was such an amazing question that I actually tried to answer it. "Why don't you call her up? Say you heard she might be going on Saturday and would she like to ride with you in your car."

He looked at me. "To painting day? Then I'd have to go. And paint."

"Duh, Willy."

"I guess it would be worth it," he said.

"She'll think it's so *sweet* of you to help the disadvantaged." I let the sarcasm drip.

"Go get your groceries." He was coming back to his senses. "Hurry up. I wanna get home and call her."

He was so nervous and excited that when we got to The Annex, he got out of the car for a change. I wasn't sure he even knew what he was doing, but I let him follow me to the shed.

It was dark, as always, but I said hello and then waited a minute for my eyes to adjust. I was used to the place now, and it didn't scare me. Gracie was lying in the corner like usual, only tonight she didn't sit up right away. She was huddled under the two thin blankets.

"Are you cold?" I asked, walking closer to her, shivering in my own down jacket.

"Cold tonight," she said quietly.

"Do you need another blanket?" What she needed was a heated place to sleep, but how could I give her that?

"You bring Gracie food?" she asked. She held out her hands to me, and I gave her the bag. Every week when I brought the food I felt bad. I kept thinking I ought to feel good, because if I didn't bring the food, nobody else would. But the bags were getting smaller—I'd used up all my dog-walking cash, and Ethan never had more than a dollar or two left over from his lunch money. Even though Willy kicked in five dollars once in a while, I still had to take money from the Emergency Jar, and I didn't want Mom to get suspicious. So I'd end up with two bananas and some bread and juice, a few little things for a whole week. I ate that much in a day.

"Do you feel all right?" I asked.

"She doesn't look so hot," Willy said from the doorway.

"You think so?"

"Skinnier than ever."

I opened the orange juice carton. "Drink some of this, Gracie."

She took the carton and drank a big swallow, spilling it down her chin.

"God, it's hard to believe she wasn't always like this," Willy said. "That she lived in a house and had a normal life."

"I know."

Gracie looked up at us guiltily. "I spilled coffee on the red rug," she said, but her mouth was curling up on the sides, becoming a little girl's smile. Suddenly she laughed out loud. "Ernest could never stay mad at me. I was too pretty!"

In the dark shed you couldn't see the blotches and wrinkles on her skin, and I got goose bumps when, just for a second, it seemed like I was seeing her young again, young and laughing.

"You still are pretty," I told her. I expected Willy to snicker in back of me, but he was quiet.

Gracie took hold of my hands, like she sometimes did. "You are my good girl. Yes sirree, you are Gracie's Girl. Yes sirree. Gracie's Girl."

We stayed awhile and watched her eat some things. It seemed like once we got there, Willy wasn't in such a big hurry to leave anymore. It's a funny thing about helping people—once you start, you get kind of addicted to it. You feel like there ought to be at least one more thing you could do. I wondered if Willy was feeling that way, too. Finally I realized it was getting late; Mom would start to wonder where we were.

"I'll bring you a better coat next week," I promised, wondering where I'd get one, since Mom had already donated all our old things to Derby Street. "Or at least another blanket," I told her. That I could get from the women's shelter donation pile.

When we left, she smiled and waved good-bye from her corner, just like a little kid when you put her to bed. Even Willy waved back. Then we pretended to lock her in, pretended she was safe, and went home.

Chapter Sixteen

Painting day was a big success, for the shelter and for Willy. For starters Caroline rode in his car with him. Then the two of them asked if they could paint one of the little bathrooms together, which meant their body parts kept bumping into each other the whole time they were in there. The giggling was quite annoying.

Ethan and I helped Harold and Jim and Newly paint the lobby. We did the walls a light creamy color, which made the dark wood around the edges look very nice. There were some guys whose real jobs were painting who Harold had talked into volunteering to paint the ceilings and all the high-up, hard stuff. They had long ladders, and they were used to doing that kind of thing without falling and killing themselves.

"I hear you two are collecting donations for the shelter at your school," Harold said.

I nodded. "We call ourselves the Women's Shelter Aid Society."

"I know your folks is proud of that," Newly said.

"You think so?" I asked. It was kind of silly, but I

wanted Newly to say more about it. I was enjoying the fact that my parents were finally noticing I was an actual human being and not just some fuzzy animal to pet once or twice a week.

"I don't think so—I know so! And now you down here painting like Picasso hisself!" Newly and Harold laughed like crazy—the two of them laughed a lot, but Jim kept right on painting like he was getting paid for it.

"You know what else we need, though?" Harold asked.

"What?"

"A good name for this place. I bet you can come up with something, couple of smart kids like you."

"Should it be something that goes with Derby Street Shelter?" Ethan asked. "Since it's just around the corner?"

"Well, it's not on Derby Street, though—we don't want to confuse people," Harold said.

"Too bad it's on South Farmington Boulevard," I said.

Everybody laughed and said at the same time, "The South Farmington Boulevard Shelter! NO!"

"We've got a week and a half until opening," Harold said. "It'd be nice to have a name by then, a name everybody will remember." Ethan and I promised to work on it.

"Harold," I said, "you know a lot of people in Atwood, don't you?"

"Well, I've lived here for all my fifty-two years, and

I love to talk, so I'd have to admit I do know lots of people."

"Did you ever meet Gracie's father when you were younger? The Reverend Matthew Jarvis?"

For a minute Harold stared at me like he was waiting for the punch line, then he burst out laughing. "Is that what Gracie told you? Sweetheart, the Reverend Matthew Jarvis was a mailman, not a minister."

"That can't be right. Gracie talks about him all the time."

"That may be, but Matthew Jarvis was a mailman just like my very own daddy. They worked together out of the South Branch office. It's a fact, my girl."

Ethan had stopped painting; he looked as disappointed as I felt. Probably we were both remembering the made-up story of the evil niece and feeling let down again.

"How am I supposed to know what's the truth and what's a lie?" I said angrily, flapping my brush against the wall hard.

Harold bent way over. "Gracie isn't lying to you, Bess. She's telling you the truth she believes. There's a big difference."

"Well, what's wrong with her, then? How come she makes up all these stories?"

Harold shook his head. "I don't know for sure. It's possible she's had a slight stroke, or some other health problem. Then again maybe her stories are just about the life she wishes she'd had, the world she'd rather live in. This one, you know, hasn't been too kind to her."

"Amen," Newly said, nodding.

Nobody laughed for a while after that. As I finished up around the old fireplace, I decided the part about the red peacock rug absolutely had to be the truth.

Mom and Dad were working in the bedrooms upstairs. Lots of people were—probably forty or fifty. There were kids from the high school—some of them more interested in slapping paint on one another than on the walls—and shelter volunteers and their friends, and at least six or seven people I recognized as Derby Street guests. They were people we'd helped out, and now they were helping us, which made me feel really good, like things were working the way they ought to.

In the middle of the morning Harold sent me upstairs with a new group of volunteers to ask Mom where they should paint. As I was on my way back downstairs, somebody called out my name from a bedroom.

"Bess! I had a feeling this might be your project, but I didn't see you when we came in." It was Suzanne, and behind her stood Anna, smiling.

It was so great to see them. "What are you guys doing down here?"

"Anna's dad knows Harold Wyman. He's a painter. He's downstairs doing the ceilings," Suzanne explained. Anna looked at the floor and chewed her cheek.

"Your dad is one of the *real* painters?" I said. "They're such a big help. Nobody else really knows how to do these high ceilings."

Anna smiled. "That's what Harold told Dad. Dad says it's impossible to say no to Harold. Then when I told Suzanne about it . . ."

"I just knew it must be the same project you were collecting money for in the cafeteria," Suzanne said, finishing Anna's sentence. "So, of course, we came, too."

Of course they came. How cool.

"We could help you collect stuff at school, too, if you want more people."

"Sure. Then Ethan and I could actually eat lunch once in a while." I laughed. "We'll talk about it on Monday, okay? I should get back to work—I have play rehearsal at one o'clock."

"Okay. See you Monday," Suzanne said.

"Thanks," Anna whispered.

As I walked back downstairs I wondered why Anna was thanking *me*. We were both volunteers. If anything, *I* should thank *her*.

Anna's little voice and the way she didn't look right at you reminded me of Janette. At least, the old Janette. I wondered if the new Janette would still want to be friends with Ethan and me. Now that she had a cute boyfriend, maybe she wouldn't want to hang around with us. After all, we spent a lot of time on the women's shelter project, which she wasn't interested in, and we'd been pronounced *dweebs* by the ultimate authority on popularity, Kimberly Pringle. Now that she wasn't so shy, Janette might want to find cooler friends.

If she did, I'd miss her. Even though Ethan and I were sort of a team, Janette had always been our good friend. She was different from us, quiet and careful and very smart. And even though she wouldn't ride bikes or hike trails with us, she always had good advice when you needed someone to talk to. We could always trust Janette. I hoped we still could. It was exciting to make new friends, like Suzanne and Anna, but I certainly didn't want to lose one of my oldest ones.

At quarter to one Mom came in with deli sandwiches for me and Ethan to eat in the car while she drove us to the middle school. We were cleaning the paint off our hands in the kitchen when I heard a voice behind me.

"Is Mrs. Cunningham here?" I couldn't believe it. It was that Mr. Atchison, the guy who sold us the hotel. What did he want? It was too late for him to make trouble now, wasn't it?

Mom came swooping over. "Mr. Atchison! I'm so happy you decided to come!"

"Well, it's not my usual sort of activity, but I can wield a paintbrush as well as the next man," he said, still looking kind of crabby. "I'm interested to see what you've done with the old place. Looks very nice, I have to say, very nice." He was looking at the cream-colored wall I'd just finished.

"We appreciate your help, Mr. Atchison. Let me set you up before I drive the kids to school." Mom led him off upstairs. "Would you rather paint the white trim or the blue walls?"

Mr. Atchison gave her a tiny smile. "You put me wherever you need me, Mrs. Cunningham. Wherever you need the work done."

Ethan and I stared at each other. My mom has this saying about how impossible projects just take a little longer to accomplish than the difficult ones. For the first time I understood what she meant.

Chapter Seventeen

What a week! Everything was going twice as fast as usual. Now that the new shelter had been painted, Mom was all excited about getting mattresses for the beds and hauling all the sheets and blankets out of our dining room and into place. There were a few articles in the local paper about what was going on, and they even mentioned the Women's Shelter Aid Society at the middle school, so more kids were bringing in donations at lunchtime. It was a good thing we had Suzanne and Anna to help.

Of course every now and then some jerk would walk by and say something lousy like, "Tell those bums to get a job—then they won't need charity," or, "If they'd stop having babies, they wouldn't need a shelter." As if big problems like this could be solved really simply, and some kid who could barely pass history had all the answers.

A few weeks ago it might have embarrassed me— people making fun of what I was doing—but not any- more. Working for the shelter was more important than having every idiot in the school like me. Besides, the kids I liked didn't care that I worked for the shelter, kids like

Suzanne and Anna. They thought it was cool. Which, I guess, just proves that there's more than one way to be cool.

Ethan's mom usually managed to pick us up after school these days because we couldn't ride our bikes home carrying a bunch of money, and sometimes there were too many blankets and things to store in the custodian's closet until Friday. It was hard for her to wrangle both little girls into car seats every afternoon, but she said she didn't mind doing it for the shelter, because the shelter had done so much for her. I didn't really know what she meant by that, except I knew she loved working at Derby Street.

Even Willy was helping us out, carting stuff over to the new shelter, although he sort of had to now, since Caroline thought he was such a terrific guy. It was amazing. He would have cooked and served dinner at Derby Street single-handedly every night of the week just to have Caroline Riley falling in love with him. Which Ethan reported that she was. We didn't discuss it too much. It made us feel icky.

In the afternoon we hurried to finish our homework and eat a little dinner. By six o'clock we had to be back at the middle school for play rehearsals, which lasted until almost ten o'clock. It was all coming together, but there were still some loose ends, which made everybody nervous. Like the lighting guy getting sick on Monday and me trying to train somebody else to get all the cues just in case he didn't get back in time. Like the elastic in the poodle skirts being too loose and falling down around the knees of the skinniest girls every time they raised their arms. Like Kimberly Pringle, who three days before opening suddenly developed stage fright.

"What if I open my mouth and nothing comes out?" she asked me, staring out into the theater as if she saw a Broadway audience of a thousand people out there.

"That won't happen," I told her, though I actually thought it might. "You've practiced for weeks. It will just be second nature once we get going."

She grabbed my arm with her sweaty hand. "I have to start the song by myself. If I don't start it, nobody else will know when to come in."

"If you don't start it, somebody else will. Just don't panic," I told her, even though I was beginning to feel a little light-headed myself.

"What if I forget the words! Sometimes when I'm nervous I forget things!" She was ready to start crying.

"Look," I said. "I'm the stage manager, right? So I'm in charge. If you forget a line, it's *my* duty to know it. Look off to the side and I'll whisper the line to you."

"Do you know all the lines?" Kimberly said, her voice full of amazement.

"I have to. Ms. Plumbly told me to memorize the whole script."

"Gosh. That *is* a big responsibility." She thought about it for a minute and then she smiled. "That does make me feel better. If I mess up, I can just blame it on you! Thanks, Bess. You're a big help!" She bounced off-stage.

The whole week was like that, one crisis after another. Then Thursday night I was running out to the car so Mom could drive Ethan and me to rehearsal, when Willy yelled out to me, "Hey, aren't you going to the library tonight?"

I stopped and stared at him. How could I have forgotten?

"Bess did her homework this afternoon," Mom said. "But I've been meaning to tell you, Willy, I think it's really wonderful the way you've been helping your sister these past few weeks. I feel like we're all working together as a family these days instead of just four people each going their own way." She gave Willy a kiss on the cheek as she walked by. He flinched a little bit, but I don't think Mom noticed.

"Mom, just a second. I need to get something," I said, and raced upstairs to Willy's room, leaping over Chesterfield, who was asleep on the stairs. Willy followed slowly.

"I totally forgot!" I said. "What can I do? I have to go to rehearsal! It's dress rehearsal, and I'm already late. And Ms. Plumbly's still mad at me for missing on Saturday!" I stamped my foot. "I can't do *everything*."

"I'll do it," Willy said, as if it was no big deal at all. "You get fruit and bread and juice, right?"

"You will? By yourself? You'll take the stuff to her?"

"She's expecting it, isn't she? You can't start to do stuff for somebody and then just forget about them."

He didn't say it as mean as it sounds, but I felt terrible, anyway. My eyes got watery.

"Hey, come on," he said. "You don't want Mom to see you bawling. Look, I go with you every week, anyway. I'll just take it in this time. I'll tell her you were busy, but you'll be there next week."

I nodded. "I said I'd bring her another blanket tonight."

"Yeah. I took one of those donated ones already. It's in the trunk."

"Tell her I'm sorry I couldn't come. Tell her by next week we can move her into the new shelter. Tell her—"

"Yeah, yeah, get going now. Mom's gonna think something's up."

"Thanks, Willy." I couldn't remember the last time I'd thanked my brother for anything.

"Go!" he ordered, and I did.

I couldn't keep my mind focused on the play that night. I kept seeing Willy walking into the dark shed by himself. For the first time I thought of Willy as a person. I mean, I'd been yapping to Janette about how all people are people and everything, but I still usually thought of Willy as some lower form of life. But that night I really liked the guy. I guess I even loved him, and it surprised me a lot.

The dress rehearsal was a mess. The lighting guy was

back, but you could hear him coughing his brains out; he was louder than the singers. The telephone girls were all late getting onstage because that stupid box of telephones had walked away again. Dara Washburne had laryngitis, and when I signaled for the curtain to come down too soon, she got caught on the wrong side of it and started crying. A tree fell over on Conrad Birdie.

Ms. Plumbly kept smiling, but every time I looked at her she was cramming another rice cake into her mouth. Her sweater was starting to look like she'd been caught in a snowstorm without a coat. "The dress rehearsal is always terrible," she kept saying. "You have to have a terrible dress to have a fabulous opening night!"

She sent us all home with little hugs and pats (I got a pat, not a hug), saying to sleep well and be there early the next evening. All would be well.

I don't know about anybody else, but I couldn't sleep a wink. First of all, I had Willy's report on Gracie.

"She was lying down again, like last time. She really needed that blanket," he said.

"Did she look sick? Did she eat anything while you were there? Did she ask about me?"

He shrugged. "How do I know if she's sick? I'm no doctor. She ate a banana, and she asked where 'Gracie's Girl' was. I told her you were busy tonight."

She really did know me! But that made me feel even worse about forgetting her. "You made it sound like I don't have time for her," I complained.

"Well, you didn't have time for her tonight," he said.

"Couldn't you have said I had a cold or something?"

"Why should I make up a lie?"

"So she doesn't get her feelings hurt!"

"Please. She's so out of it, she doesn't know what I said." He acted like he was mad he'd done a nice thing. Just when I was starting to like him.

"That's not true, Willy. Take it back!"

"Look, I did you a favor and I did her a favor. Don't make me wish I hadn't!" He slammed the door to his room, and I went off to spend a sleepless night worrying about old ladies, leading ladies, and a box of telephones with a mind of its own.

Chapter Eighteen

This was it—the big weekend. Friday in school I couldn't concentrate on one thing. I noticed in English class that Kimberly Pringle was absent, and I tried not to imagine the disaster that was keeping her home.

"Her mother is probably letting her stay home to get her beauty rest or something," Ethan said.

"I just hope her mother isn't sewing her a new costume," I said. Mrs. Pringle had not been happy that her daughter's costume was the same as all the other teenage characters'. Mrs. Pringle thought Kimberly was the star of the show, and nobody was going to convince her otherwise. You could see where Kimberly got her attitude.

Still, I was surprised when I showed up at the auditorium that night to find Kimberly prancing around in three-inch heels, with rhinestones sewn all over her white sweater. Ms. Plumbly was having a fit.

"All the girls have to be in the same outfit, Kimberly. That's why we have dress rehearsal—to do a final costume check. You can't just decide to wear something else the night of the play! High heels are not appropriate for a musical about the fifties. The girls all wear sneakers and bobby socks!"

"But bobby socks are so unattractive, don't you think?" Mrs. Pringle asked, looking around at all of us. "They make your legs look chunky."

"That is not the issue," Ms. Plumbly said. "We're doing *Bye Bye Birdie*, not *A Chorus Line*."

"The heels make Kimberly stand out from the crowd, as she should. She's the third-most important female role," Mrs. Pringle explained to Ms. Plumbly.

If I thought I'd seen Ms. Plumbly angry before, it was nothing compared to this. She pulled herself up tall and looked down on Kimberly's mother. "Mrs. Pringle, listen to what I'm saying. I am the director of this play, which means, what I say goes. Kimberly will wear the same outfit as the other teenage characters, as she did yesterday for the dress rehearsal. No heels. And I would appreciate it if you would remove the rhinestones from her sweater right now."

"And what if I refuse?" Mrs. Pringle said sweetly.

Ms. Plumbly stared at Mrs. Pringle. "Then the understudy will play Ursula," she said. (Heidi Cohen gave a little gasp—she'd only rehearsed the part once, but Kimberly's mother didn't know that.)

Mrs. Pringle's face twisted into a little knot. "I see." She stuck her head up in the air and went to tell the news to Kimberly, who was flouncing around showing herself off.

"I don't really care," Kimberly said, kicking off the heels. "I can't walk in these things, anyway."

After that it was pretty smooth sailing. Everything

went fine, just like Ms. Plumbly had predicted it would. Well, maybe not *everything*. The orchestra did drown out Dara's weak voice, but the telephones didn't run away, and nobody's clothes fell off, and the audience laughed like crazy. When it was all over, they stood up and applauded for about five minutes. Of course, the audience was made up entirely of parents and friends of the cast, so we sort of expected that, but it made us feel good, anyway. I couldn't wait to do it again tomorrow.

I was so exhausted, it was noon before I got out of bed the next day. It was pouring down rain and really cold out. I was glad Willy had taken the extra blanket to Gracie. The wind howled around the corners of the house like we were in the middle of a horror movie.

I hoped Gracie would stay in The Annex all day, but I wasn't sure if she knew which days were weekends. Every day probably seemed about the same to her. I wondered if she'd gone to the supermarket this morning to check out the Dumpster. I doubted that Ethan had gotten up early enough to find her down there, either; besides, his mother wouldn't have let him ride his bike so far in this weather, anyway.

And then I started to feel a little mad. After all, I was just a kid. I had lots of things to do in my life. The play was important, too, like Ms. Plumbly said. I couldn't spend every minute worrying about Gracie. She'd be all right for another week. I'd go see her next Wednesday night, just before Thanksgiving, and tell her about staying in the shelter. I could probably talk Willy into driving her over on Thursday for the opening. Then she wouldn't need The Annex anymore. She wouldn't need *me* anymore. I'd still see her, of course, but it would be a relief not to feel so responsible for her.

Ethan came over in the afternoon, and we talked about the play. What we'd do a little differently tonight, to keep things running smoothly backstage. Ethan is good under pressure; he always stays calm.

And then it was showtime again. Saturday night was even better than Friday. Mom and Dad came, and Willy and Caroline came, too, and Ethan's parents. When the play was over, Ms. Plumbly came up onstage and read off the names of all the backstage people, and we came out to take a bow. She made a big deal about what a great stage manager I was, which was really nice, considering that argument we'd had last week. It was kind of scary to stand out there on the stage and have the whole audience looking at you. I had about fifteen seconds of stage fright myself.

As we were all filing off the stage, I pulled Ms. Plumbly aside. "I'm sorry about last Saturday. I know you think the play should have been my first commitment, but when two things are important, it's hard to know which to put first. I wanted to do them both."

She put her hand on my shoulder. "I understand that, Bess. But I was so nervous last week, it made me angry that you seemed to be choosing the shelter project over the play. I felt you were deserting me."

"I know and I'm sorry. If I promise never to do it again, do you think I could be stage manager again sometime?"

She laughed. "Don't make promises you may not be able to keep. Bess, you were a very good stage manager and, for the most part, very reliable. Consider yourself forgiven. I hope you and Ethan will both want to work with me again. As a matter of fact, I'll be very annoyed if you don't!"

"Oh, we do! We will!" I gave her a hug from the front just as Kimberly Pringle came flying at her from the rear, making a Plumbly sandwich.

"This was such a wonderful experience, Ms. Plumbly," Kimberly said. "I just can't wait to do it again!" Ms. Plumbly had a look on her face that seemed to say she could, personally, stand to wait a little while.

Afterward we felt like stars or something. People we hardly knew came up and hugged us and said what a great job we'd done. I noticed that Jake brought flowers for Janette. They stood in the corner and held hands; I pretended not to see them.

Mom and Dad brought me flowers, too, small yellow roses. Even Willy said, "Good job," which is about all you could expect from him. Ethan and I went to the cast party, where everybody was screaming and crying and laughing and hugging each other, like that lousy dress rehearsal had never happened, like we were all crazy about one another, like we were different people than we had been two days ago, or would be again on Monday morning. It was great.

I decided I could definitely get used to having people

pay attention to me. Especially if I could do it without wearing a hat!

On Sunday I woke up to find that I was Queen for a Day because of doing such a good job stage-managing the play and simultaneously working on the shelter project. I've had it happen a few times before. Everybody in the family has. I don't know how it got started—it was probably before I was born—but if one of us really deserves a celebration, if you've done something outstanding, you get to be King or Queen for a Day. The others just get together and decide it. You never know about it beforehand: It's a surprise.

Once Willy was King for a Day when he helped some neighborhood kid find his lost dog. That's the only time I remember him getting it, and it was a while ago, but he probably got it more when he was a little kid. These days Willy's not exactly the Kingly type. Although I thought he ought to get it for taking the food and blanket to Gracie when I couldn't and for not making a big deal about it. Maybe once the shelter was open, I'd tell Mom the whole story and Willy could make King again.

I got Queen one time after I made the only goal I ever scored in three years of playing soccer. And one other time I got it because Mom broke her leg, and Willy and I were supposed to clean up the kitchen after dinner every night, and Willy complained about it constantly, but, for some reason, I didn't. Willy didn't think it was fair I got

Queen for a Day that time, but he was outvoted. So he refused to bow when I walked by like you're supposed to.

Dad got King when he made partner in his law firm, and one time for finally fixing the porch railing that had been broken for about five years. Mom has made it a bunch of times, though she always says she doesn't deserve it, don't make a fuss. But it's fun to do King and Queen for a Day even if you aren't the one who gets it. It's fun because it's just our family, all together, doing nice things for one another.

First of all, the royal person can choose to do anything they want to all day, within certain legal limits, of course, and everybody has to go along with them. They choose what to eat, too, and it can be all sugar if they want, or all-day pizza, which is what Willy chose that one time.

I always like breakfast in bed, so Sunday morning Dad surprised me with it—strawberry pancakes, bacon, and homemade cocoa, my favorite things. It was the day we were supposed to go to the shelter to serve lunch, but Mom got a bunch of her high school students to go instead. She said it would be good for them to spend the day with Harold, and it would good for us to spend a quiet day together at home for a change—which sounded great to me. We'd all be at the ceremony for the new shelter on Thursday morning, anyway, and we'd be serving a turkey dinner at Derby Street in the middle of the afternoon.

It was a perfect day. Mom went to the video store and rented some old Cary Grant movies, which I love, and we watched them all afternoon. Dad made a fire in the fireplace while I made popcorn with lots of butter. It was still rainy, so we couldn't do anything outside, but I didn't really want to, anyway. I didn't even get dressed, just sat around in my pajamas and bathrobe all day. Even Willy stayed home, although he talked to Caroline on the telephone for about three hours.

We had tacos for supper, my choice, and then put on some old music from when Mom and Dad were young. Dad loves to dance, and he's taught me lots of steps. Mom will dance, too, if he forces her, but tonight he mostly danced with me. It had been so long since we'd had a day like this, all of us together and relaxed, nobody late for anything or worried about what time it was.

I was about ready to go upstairs to bed when Mom suddenly remembered. "Names!" she said. "The ceremony is only four days away, and we still don't have a name for the new shelter. Let's put our heads together for a few minutes and see if we can come up with something. Harold said he was hoping you and Ethan would come up with a name," she reminded me.

"We've been so busy with the play," I said. "Besides, I don't know how to name a building."

"I think we should name it after you," Dad told Mom. "The Alice Estes Cunningham Shelter."

"Oh, please, no," Mom said, waving her hand in front

of her face. "It sounds like I'm dead. Besides, so many other people worked on the project, too."

"How about something like the End of the Road House," Willy said. "That's poetic."

"It's pathetic!" I said. "Who wants to go to the End of the Road?"

"It does sound a little dismal, Willy," Mom agreed. "I thought maybe the Emerson Shelter. Since that was the name of the hotel. That way people would know where it is."

"Well, it's not catchy, but it would serve the purpose," Dad said.

"The Hungry Hotel. The Cheap Sleep," Willy said, laughing at his own stupid jokes.

"Keep thinking," Mom said, giving him the evil eye. "Maybe the perfect thing will strike us before Thursday."

It wasn't until bedtime that I remembered Gracie—I hadn't given her a thought all weekend, which made me feel a little guilty. I hoped she hadn't gotten too wet the last few days. Tomorrow after school Jake and some other kids planned to move the *Bye Bye Birdie* flats back to The Zone Annex. Ethan had said he'd help, too, so he could try to scoot Gracie's blankets and other stuff out of the way, and also make sure there was still enough room for her to sleep there. There had to be. In just a few more nights she could move to the shelter; then we wouldn't have to worry about her anymore.

Chapter Nineteen

It was sunny the next morning and unusually warm for November, which was especially nice after the crummy weekend weather, so Ethan and I decided to ride our bikes to school again. Pretty soon the weather would make it impossible, and we wanted to take advantage of the final good days.

As soon as the school came into sight, I knew something was wrong. Everything looked different from usual. All the kids were gathered on the side of the building by the parking lot instead of spread around the whole front yard. The closer we got, the weirder it was. Too quiet. Not like other mornings.

As we pulled our bikes into the driveway, I saw what the kids were gathered around: an ambulance. And then I knew. I just knew it right then.

"It's Gracie. Something's happened to Gracie!"

Ethan ditched his bike and started running. I was right behind him.

But by the time we got close to the ambulance, the attendant had shut the doors already.

"What happened?" Ethan shouted. "Who was it?"

"I heard it was some old bag lady," a girl said. "They found her back by that shed."

"What was wrong with her?" I said.

The girl shrugged. "They had a blanket over her face. Doesn't that mean you're dead?"

Dead? That couldn't be right. She didn't know what she was talking about. But Mrs. Falucci, the principal, was outside by then, trying to calm everybody down.

"I want you all to file into the auditorium. I know it's upsetting to see something like this, and I want to talk to you about it," she said. Kids started heading inside. Everybody was noisy now. The crisis was over, plus they were getting out of their first-period classes.

But Ethan and I stood outside, listening to the ambulance siren roar away into silence.

"They wouldn't turn on the siren if she was dead, would they?" Ethan asked me.

"I don't know," I said miserably. "How could she be dead? She was fine. I mean, not *fine,* but she was okay. I took her food. Willy took her food Thursday night. She couldn't die that fast, could she?"

"I don't know much about dying," Ethan said. He looked worried, though.

Almost everybody had gone inside, and some of the teachers were going around getting the last of us to come in. The assembly was starting.

Mrs. Falucci stood up. "Because so many of you were witnesses to this morning's events, I felt we should talk about

170

it a little. When Mr. Lucas, the custodian, came to work this morning, he found an elderly woman lying outside near The Zone Annex shed by the parking lot. She was . . . dead."

I grabbed Ethan's arm and let the tears fall down my cheeks. I didn't want to hear any more, but I couldn't leave, either.

"Apparently the woman was a transient, someone without a home. We think she may have been using the shed as a place to sleep. Without knowing that, of course, Mr. Lucas put new locks on the shed over the weekend."

New locks! She couldn't get in! Ethan stamped his foot, over and over. He was trying to keep from crying, too, I guess, but it didn't work.

"It's a sad commentary on our society," Mrs. Falucci continued, "that there are people who have no home, that tragedies like this can happen."

This isn't just some tragedy you read about in the newspaper! I wanted to scream at her. *This is Gracie! Gracie, who trusted me, who said I was her good girl, Gracie's Girl!*

I looked at the kids sitting near me; Gracie's death meant hardly anything to them. They were whispering to one another, or finishing up their homework. One boy was taking a snooze. I knew they were all happy to be in assembly instead of in class—a change from the usual schedule is always good, and a little exciting, and besides, the whole thing had nothing to do with them.

Mrs. Falucci kept talking. "But even in the midst of our sorrow, we should remember that there are people working to rectify these problems. The new women's shelter will be opening on Thursday. This Thanksgiving we should thank people like our own Bess Cunningham and Ethan Riley, who have been collecting donations for the shelter for over a month. They are proof to us that everyone can make a difference."

It was the most horrible moment of my life. Everybody turned around to look at us, me and Ethan, thinking we'd done some great thing. Mrs. Falucci started to clap, and the kids joined in, some of them yelling, "Yay, Bess! Yay, Ethan!"

It was the kind of thing I had always wanted to have happen to me. Everybody knowing who I was and thinking I was terrific. Except I wasn't, and neither was Ethan. In fact, we'd probably killed Gracie ourselves. If we hadn't gotten her to come and stay in the shed, she'd probably still be alive! If we hadn't gotten so caught up with the play over the weekend, we might have checked on her and realized something was wrong!

Of course everybody thought we were crying because we were so upset about some old lady we didn't even know. They had no idea. I saw Janette sitting down in front with Jake. She knew. She turned around and looked at us, too, like she felt sorry for us. But it wasn't us she ought to be feeling sorry for.

I walked straight out of the assembly to the pay phone in the hall and called my mom, who'd just arrived at work at the high school. I was crying so hard, I could barely speak. "Mom! Gracie's dead! They just took her away in an ambulance, and it's my fault!"

She didn't know what I was talking about, but I sounded so bad, she said she'd come right over. Ethan and I both got excused for the day and sat in the principal's office to wait for her.

Mrs. Falucci waited with us and kept saying how compassionate we were and everything. I thought I might throw up. But I managed to survive until Mom came in, and Mrs. Falucci told her version of what had happened and got finished praising us one more time. And then we got out of the building, and I fell apart.

Ethan was crying again, too, so Mom made us stop and sit on a wall near the cafeteria to talk. Luckily nobody eats lunch that early, so we didn't have an audience.

"It might not have been Gracie," Mom said. "Unfortunately, there are other homeless old women, too."

I shook my head. "It was her, Mom. We brought her here. We thought it was a safe place." Then I told her the whole story, about Willy driving Gracie to The Zone Annex, and Willy and me bringing her food and blankets, and about how I was planning to nominate him for King for a Day, and then about the new locks and how she wouldn't have been able to get into her little house.

"Let's go home," Mom said, putting an arm around each of us. "I'll call the hospital and Harold. We'll make sure. Although it sounds like you're right." She didn't yell at us or anything, but I could tell she was feeling awful, too.

Ethan and I sat on the sofa, looking at our hands while Mom made phone calls. Some of it we could understand just from listening to her half of the conversation. Harold had already been called by the hospital. He'd had to go down and identify Gracie's body. It was her all right. When she got all the information, Mom came and sat down on the coffee table right in front of us.

"I talked to a doctor. He said Gracie died of heart failure. The hospital had some old records on her, from before, when her husband was still alive, before she was homeless. Apparently she's had heart trouble for years, and was once on medication, but I don't suppose she'd taken it for quite some time. According to their records she was only sixty-six years old."

Ethan looked up. "That's pretty old."

Mom smiled sadly. "Well, not so old. People can live to be much older with proper care. That's why we need a clinic down by the shelters. That's the next thing we've got to do. A free clinic, so these people don't have to suffer so much." Even though her eyes were teary, too, I could see she was already thinking ahead, past Gracie, on to the next problem.

But I was stuck back at The Zone Annex. I kept thinking of Gracie trying to get in and not understanding about the new locks. Ethan sighed deeply, so he was probably thinking the same thing.

"I wish you guys had told me what you were doing," Mom said gently. "I understand why you didn't, but these

174

problems are too difficult for children your age to deal with alone."

I had to ask her; I hoped she'd tell me the truth. "Did we kill her?" I said, and then burst out crying again.

"Oh, Bess, no! Of course not, sweetheart." Mom came and sat next to me then and hugged me. "Don't ever think that! You did what you thought was best, and it probably *was* the best thing, under the circumstances. Otherwise, she'd have been sleeping outside all these months! You sheltered her and fed her for almost two months. She probably wouldn't have lived as long as she did without your help."

"You really think so?" I said, shivering, even though I hadn't taken off my heavy jacket all morning.

"I'm sure of it. You and Ethan were her guardian angels."

"And Willy," I added, sniffling.

"And, amazingly enough, Willy," she said.

"But if they hadn't changed the locks," Ethan said, "she'd probably still be alive. If we'd checked over the weekend . . . we were so busy . . . she only had four more days until the shelter opened."

"Ethan, Bess. Look at me. The two of you have done a great deal to help so many people. Believe me, I understand how you feel. I've felt this way so often over the years—the problems are so large, you begin to feel hopeless yourself. As much as you do, there's still so much more you weren't able to do. But you have to concentrate on what you *are* accomplishing, not what you aren't.

"Now, I called your mother, Ethan, and explained the whole thing," Mom told him. "She's waiting for you, and she said she'd have hot cocoa made by the time you got there."

He nodded. "Okay. Thanks, Mrs. Cunningham." We waved to each other as he left, but we couldn't find the right words to say out loud.

"Would you like me to make you some cocoa, too?" Mom asked.

"No, I just want you to sit here with me for a while," I said. "I feel so bad."

"I know, honey. I do, too. I should have been keeping track of her all these months. I'm a social worker—I knew she was all alone. But I was so focused on the new shelter, I didn't think about what was happening to people in the meantime."

"What could you have done?" I asked her.

"Good question. Maybe I should have brought Gracie here, to our house, for those months. That would have been hard on all of us, but if I'd known how sick she was, I might have. Of course, I can't bring *everybody* home. As long as I've worked in this field, it's still sometimes hard for me to figure out what's the right thing to do. How do you choose who needs you more?"

I curled my legs up under me and leaned into her side. "Right now, I need you more," I told her.

"Oh, Bess," she said, her tears rolling fast now, "I need you, too, honey. I need you, too."

Chapter Twenty

Mom stayed home all day. We played Scrabble and Boggle, and sat together on the couch to watch *Rosie*. We talked about all kinds of things we don't usually have time to talk about, like what my favorite course is in school (history), and Grandma and Grandpa Estes, who live far away (Minnesota), and whether I remembered the cat we had before Chesterfield (Hilda—not really). Just talking made me feel a little better.

Then Mom made fried chicken for dinner, which she almost never does, and mashed potatoes, to cheer everybody up. But Willy and I couldn't eat much. He acted mad. He was even swearing, which normally Mom and Dad would not have allowed at the dinner table, but tonight they let it go. It was like he was mad for all of us.

"Dammit! Why did they have to change the locks *now?*" he said, even though Mom had explained that it probably wasn't being outside at night that had killed Gracie. "Didn't anybody even look inside first? Just to *check?* They would have seen her stuff!"

"It was a storage shed, Willy," Dad said. "Mr. Lucas didn't expect anyone to be sleeping there."

"Well, dammit, he should have *checked!*" Willy insisted. Nobody felt like arguing with him.

There was an article about Gracie in the paper on Tuesday, and about the new women's shelter opening, too. Wednesday was the last day Ethan and I were planning to set up our collection table for the shelter, and we got flooded. Lots more sheets and blankets, which were still needed, but even better, lots of money. Every kid who watched the ambulance take Gracie away must have gotten their parents to write a check. We were glad to get all the donations, but it was lousy that Gracie had to die to get everybody to pay attention.

Wednesday night there was a memorial service for Gracie at Derby Street. We all went: our whole family, and most of Ethan's except for his little sisters. I'd only been to a funeral service once before, when my grandma Cunningham died. And even though that was in a fancy funeral home and this one was in a homeless shelter, it didn't seem too different.

A lot of the Derby Street regulars were there, and I recognized some of the Sunday volunteers, too. It was a pretty big crowd, considering nobody had seemed to care too much about Gracie while she was alive. The nicest part was that Newly had gotten some of the choir singers together, including Audrey and Jim, and, of course, John Bailey, because he sings better than most people you hear on the radio, and they did a few hymns. I asked if they knew how to sing "Rock of Ages" because I knew Gracie had liked that song, so they finished up with that one.

I kept thinking about my grandmother, and how I'd cried at her funeral because she'd never make pancakes with chocolate chips for me anymore, or sing "Skinny-Marink-a-Dink-a-Dink" to me just before bed. And then for a minute I got confused and thought it *was* my grandmother who'd just died. But then I remembered that it was Gracie who was dead, who'd called me her girl because I'd brought her a few measly apples and some bread once a week, not my grandmother with her beautiful white hair, who never in her life had to sleep in a shed or eat out of a Dumpster.

I wasn't the only person crying puddles. Lots of people were leaking all over the place. Willy stood in the back holding Caroline Riley's hand. Even she was crying, although she'd never actually met Gracie, and Willy was having to twist his face into a crooked snarl and chomp down on his cheek in order to keep the eyewash inside.

The surprise of the night was to see Mr. Atchison, the ex-owner of the Emerson Hotel, standing near the door, probably so he could make a quick escape if he had to. He looked sad, though, and I had to remind myself, people are all people.

There was a minister there from our church, but, of course, he didn't really know Gracie, so Mom and Harold both got up, too, and said nice things about her. At the end of her speech, Mom said she hoped everyone would come to the opening of the new shelter tomorrow at noon, after which there would be a turkey dinner served at Derby Street.

"For some of us, Grace Jarvis Battle was our inspiration for opening a shelter for women here in Atwood. And although she won't be with us tomorrow, we won't forget her. It was my daughter, Bess, who suggested the obvious name for our new shelter, and the most fitting memorial for a fine woman. Please join us at noon tomorrow for the opening of Gracie's Place."

Everybody applauded, and Dad put his arm around me. It made me feel a little better that Gracie wouldn't be forgotten now or for a long time to come.

Thanksgiving Day was almost like a celebration. Harold had gotten some kids to paint a big wooden sign that said, GRACIE'S PLACE in green letters that looked like a vine with leaves that twisted through the letters. It was beautiful. When I first saw it, I had to sniff a little bit more. Here it was, Gracie's new home, and she wasn't even here to see it.

I guess Mom knew what I was thinking. She rubbed my back. "I know. I miss her, too," she said.

We couldn't stay sad for long, though. So many people showed up! Kids I'd seen at the middle school but didn't know too well came with their folks. Suzanne came with Anna and her dad. And kids from the play came, some who had worked on the stage crew with me, and some actors, too. Even Dara Washburne was there—with Mitchell Montana! She gave me a hug, like it was opening night all over again.

We stood around in the cream-colored lobby, which had been all cleaned and polished for today. It looked like a fancy hotel again. There were already women in a line at the front desk signing up for a room for the night. Ellie MacNamara and Petey were right up front. A volunteer was writing down names, and little kids were running around touching everything, like they couldn't believe they were going to stay there. Mom had some of the kids from the high school giving tours upstairs to show all the rooms fitted out with their clean sheets and donated blankets. The place looked good.

Mom and Harold each gave another short speech, and everybody cheered for them. Mom said we couldn't sit back and rest. The shelter was wonderful, but now we should work toward starting a free clinic in the downtown area, and a day care center, too, so women could work and get their families out of poverty.

"Let's start a tutoring program for the children down here!" Harold said when it was his turn. It was like one idea was turning into a dozen. And everybody was excited to get going on them. I was, too, even though it probably meant no more long talks with Mom for a while, and a dining-room table piled high with something other than dinner.

When the speeches were finished, there was punch to drink, and plates of cold cuts and cheese and bread that Mom had gotten that grouchy supermarket manager to donate. And, of course, there was a lot more next door at Derby Street, where Harold and Dad had put the turkeys in the oven early in the morning.

Lots of people came up to me and Ethan and told us we'd done a great job helping with donations. In fact, several kids asked if they could join the Women's Shelter Aid Society. Ethan and I had figured we'd close down our operations once the shelter was actually open, but since we had so many kids interested in it now, we decided we might as well keep it going to help out with all the new projects. Only now we'd call it Gracie's Friends.

The biggest surprise of the day was hearing this little voice behind me, a voice I hadn't heard in weeks. "Hi, Bess," it said.

I turned around. "Hi, Janette. I never expected to see you here."

"I know. I'm sorry about Gracie. I'm sorry about . . . everything."

I shrugged. "It's okay." It's not that I wasn't happy to see her—I was really happy. But I wasn't sure if we were still friends, now that she was getting sort of cool and everything. I didn't want to make a big deal about her being there.

She took a deep breath. "You've been so busy with the play, I haven't even seen you lately."

"Yeah, well, I guess you've been busy, too. With Jake and all."

She blushed. "Is that why you don't want to be my friend anymore? Because of Jake? Is that why you're mad at me?"

I was shocked. "*Me?* I'm not mad. I just thought you wanted to hang around with other kids now. Jake's friends, and . . . cooler kids."

She laughed. "You're about the coolest person I can handle, Bess. Anybody cooler than you and Ethan makes me break out in hives."

"Well, then, you must be as itchy as Chesterfield in flea season!" It was so great to be able to laugh with Janette again. I was glad I wouldn't have to miss her, too. Just then Ethan walked up with Jake, and I had to look away. Why did I have to feel this way about Janette's boyfriend?

"Hi, Bess," Jake said. I couldn't help but flinch; I was sure I'd never heard him say my name before.

My tongue tied itself into a big fat knot in my mouth. I barely managed a garbled, "Hiya."

"Janette told me the whole story about you guys hiding that old woman Gracie in The Zone Annex all these weeks. I could hardly believe it." He shook his head. "I wish I'd known. I wouldn't have kept after Mr. Lucas about that lock."

"Would you have let her stay?" I blurted out. Much as I liked Jake, I didn't think of him as particularly soft-hearted.

"Well, I don't think I'd have moved her in there myself, but if I'd found out she was already there, and the circumstances and everything, I wouldn't have told anyone or made her leave. I feel awful about her dying right outside the door."

"She didn't die because of being outside," Ethan told him. "She had a heart problem and she wasn't taking any medicine for it."

Jake nodded. "Still, I feel bad."

"We all do," I said.

It was nice to be talking to Jake as a friend. He hardly seemed like the same moody guy who had ordered everybody around down in The Zone. Which was good, because I wasn't so nervous talking to him if he acted like a regular person.

"You know, I really like taking on big projects," he said. "If you need any more help with this shelter thing, sign me up." Janette was standing right next to him, as if it was her spot, as if she owned the air rights to his body. I wished that didn't make me feel so crummy—I'd just have to get used to it, because if I was really Janette's friend, I couldn't be miserably jealous every time she stood next to her boyfriend. Maybe I could find some other boy to be crazy about instead, if I put my mind to it.

Ethan told Jake about Gracie's Friends, and right away he wanted to be part of it. If I know Jake (which I don't, really), he'll probably want to take it over and run the whole thing, but we won't let him. After all, Ethan and I are the stage managers!

"This place isn't so bad, is it?" Janette said. "I mean, it's not weird or anything, like I thought it would be."

"Of course it isn't," Jake said. "Sometimes you let your mother's imagination run away with you." Usually Janette doesn't take too well to people making fun of her mother, even though she complains about her all the time herself, but apparently Jake can get away with it.

"It's funny," Ethan said after Janette and Jake had wandered off to get more punch. "A couple of months ago you were dressing up in feathers and scarves and planning how to be friends with the popular kids. And now we've got a bunch of new friends, anyway, without you wearing that silly stuff. Really nice friends, like Harold and Newly and Jim and . . ."

"Suzanne and Anna and Jake," I said.

"And even Willy, sort of," Ethan continued. "Are you doing King for a Day for him tomorrow?"

"Shh!" I said, looking around to make sure he wasn't nearby. "It's a surprise. Mom and Dad were all for it. We're having pizza for breakfast—you and Caroline should come over!"

"Pizza for breakfast! What time does he get up?"

Just then Harold came up behind us. "I need two hale and hearty young folks to cut out two hundred fifty of my special-recipe sourdough biscuits. And if you help, you get to taste-test the first ones out of the oven!"

Who could resist an offer like that? I told Mom where we were headed. Then Ethan and I followed Harold over to the Derby Street Shelter, where the smells of Thanksgiving—turkey, dressing, cranberries, and pumpkin—were strong enough and sweet enough to give anybody hope.